AF571714

Middle Eastern Memories

Middle Eastern Memories

Samyr Souki

VANTAGE PRESS
New York

FIRST EDITION

Published by Vantage Press, Inc.
516 West 34th Street, New York, New York 10001

Manufactured in the United States of America
ISBN:0-533-10181-6

Library of Congress Catalog Card No.: 91-91539

0 9 8 7 6 5 4 3 2 1

To my wife, Nicole

Contents

Preface

The latter part of World War II brought with it the resumption of a different kind of conflict in the Middle East—the struggle, started late in the nineteenth century, for independence.

Simultaneously came the entry of Soviet Russia into the picture and an intensified political struggle between the Big Four.

The Middle East generally means the Arab world and Iran. The Arab world includes Egypt, Palestine, Transjordan, Lebanon, Syria, Iraq, Saudi Arabia, Yemen, and North Africa. The combined population totals some ninety million people.

This part of the world has seen more unrest since 1943 than any other one area.

It is the fight of the underdog for a place in the sun, the one-time subject races throwing off the shackles of colonialism and striking out on their own.

These chapters, by no means a complete picture, are designed to give an idea of the Middle East—its people, their makeup, dreams, ambitions, achievements, and shortcomings. They also sketch briefly the importance of the area to the Great Powers and of their clashing interests. The period that I will be discussing runs from 1943 to 1956 when Britain, France, and Israel attacked Egypt.

Both the increasing bid for freedom of the Middle Easterners and the rivalry of the powers have tremendous significance for common people everywhere. Either or both of these factors may well be the spark that will kindle a third world war.

Today, the world must know its Middle East. Common

people everywhere must know what makes the Middle East tick. Because if they don't, and maybe even if they do, many may find themselves buried in some battlefield in the area. So perhaps it is a good idea to get acquainted with this explosive part of the world.

I have been fortunate to be able to follow almost every movement of importance in the Middle East from close quarters during the period following World War II to the midfifties. My then job as correspondent in this area took me to every Middle Eastern country whenever major events were taking place.

The French coup in Lebanon, the birth of the Arab League, the troubles in Palestine, the shelling of Damascus, the new kingdom of Transjordan, changing Saudi Arabia and its oil, the Russian threat to Iran, the struggle of nationalist Egypt, and the Iraqi crises were part of the picture.

All this followed the most dramatic phase of war and its aftermath. A badly prepared Arab world, exploited by inexperienced leaders and ill-equipped, marched in a ''Jihad'' against the Zionist settlers. They were thrown back. Embittered by defeat, they turned against the Western nations, whom they accused of aiding the Jews against the Arabs. But they also turned against their own leaders. The thrones of kings toppled, and great movements rose. The fate of nations hung in the balance. Cairo was burned by a furious mob. Farouk was thrown out of Egypt. Abdullah of Jordan was shot. His son was locked up in an asylum. El Khoury of Lebanon was pushed out. His premier, Riad el Solh, was killed. In Syria, there was a succession of upheavals. Leaders were exiled or cut down.

From the ranks rose new men, new faces. They had clean records and accepted the challenge of the times. To the corrupt among them, and to the outdated European nations, they threw down the gauntlet. They fought friends and allies, but as equals, not as underdogs.

My information has been gathered mainly by eyewitnessing

events and talking to kings, emirs, sheikhs, prime ministers, generals, underground leaders, foreign diplomats, American and British agents, and the common people of these countries. I knew little about the whole business when it started in 1943. The background I got from history books.

But perhaps the most important pages of this history were those being written in blood and intrigue before my very eyes.

The story is still unfolding. To understand what has happened in the forty years after the end of World War II—and is still happening—it is useful to remember the first years when it all started.

Middle Eastern Memories

I
Lebanon—1943

The trucks, loaded with French marines and Senegalese Negro troops, screeched to a halt in front of the modest villa of the president of Lebanon. Before the startled Lebanese sentries could do anything, they were disarmed.

Led by a French officer, the Senegalese troops scrambled up the marble steps into the main hall and upstairs into the bedroom of Sheikh Beshara el Khoury, the president of the tiny little republic nestling in the southeastern corner of the Mediterranean. The French officer, revolver in hand, said curtly, "Get dressed and put some warm clothes in a bag. By order of the French high commissioner, you are under arrest."

Outside the room, the president's ailing wife, Mrs. Laure el Khoury, stood trembling, with one protecting arm flung around her daughter Huguette, as the Senegalese gaily plundered the house. Other soldiers were cheerfully slapping seventeen-year-old Sheikh Khalil, the president's elder son, who had tried desperately to reach his father's side.

Meanwhile, in other parts of the Lebanese capital of Beirut, similar scenes were taking place as French and Senegalese troops, acting on orders from Monsieur Jean Helleu, the French high commissioner, were arresting the members of the Lebanese Cabinet and two other popular leaders

Senegalese troops moved into the home of Riad Bey Solh, Muslim prime minister of Lebanon, and snatched him away from his wife's side.

By dawn, November 11, 1943, when Beirut opened her eyes, the French had posted tanks, armored cars, and troops in all strategic areas of the city and had taken over control of the capital.

Only two ministers had escaped arrest: Vice-Premier Habib Abi Shahla, a cigar-smoking, bespectacled politician, and Emir Majid Arslan, minister of defence, had both taken to the hills and were in hiding.

Thus the fighting for freedom in the Arab world entered a new phase. The world, which had first heard of the struggle for Arab independence when the notorious Lawrence of Arabia raised an army to fight Turks and Germans in the First World War, started to hear again of Arabs crying and dying for their freedom. True, during the early years of the Second World War, the eyes of all had been turned to the Middle East, but the comparatively smaller issues of Arab freedom were lost as Allies and Axis fought in the lands that had cradled civilization.

In 1943, though the world war was still on, it had swept away from the Middle East, pursuing its deadly course through Europe and the Far East.

In the lands of the Arabs, a new war had started—a war that was to have happy and tragic results for many nations, a war that ultimately dragged the whole United Nations into the muddle. At times it was a shooting war; at others, a cold one.

The first physical blow in this new phase was struck on November 11, 1943, in Beirut, Lebanon, after the arrest of President El Khoury and his government. Angry Lebanese citizens heard the news at dawn and rushed into the streets. They overturned French cars and pulled down pictures of General de Gaulle, leader of Free France. The first shots were fired and the first few Arabs died that day.

But to understand the events of November 11, we must go back to June 8, 1941, when British, Australian, and Free French troops crossed into Lebanon from Palestine to fight the Vichy French, then in control of the country.

Lebanon was a tiny republic in the Eastern Mediterranean with a population of just over 1 million. A little more than half the inhabitants were Christians, the rest mainly Muslims and about 200,000 Druze tribesmen. This country is the land of the ancient Phoenicians, those adventurous sailors and traders whose commerce took them as far as the shores of England. They invented the alphabet some three thousand years before our times.

A great deal of the world's decisive events are written on the stone slabs on the mountain slopes of Lebanon. Many conquerors came and went over the centuries until, at long last, the end of the First World War saw Lebanon become a French mandate. Between them, France and Britain had carved up the Middle East in 1920, and the mandatory system had come into being.

The two decades separating the First and Second World Wars saw troubles, riots, and reprisals as Arab nationalists unsuccessfully tried to obtain their independence. By the Second World War, the Arab countries were coveted by both Allies and Axis. Thus started the fight for the Middle East. While armies faced each other on the sandy battlefields of the Western desert, agents of all the fighting powers were prowling around the bazaars of the Arab capitals, intriguing, lining up allies, and making every kind of promise in return for Arab support.

In Europe, the phoney war came to an end. In fifteen days, France was occupied by the Germans. The French Empire was undecided. Wherever Frenchmen were, the same question arose—de Gaulle or Vichy? In the Levant—Syria and Lebanon—there was a fair-sized French army under the command of General Dentz. Most of them had sided with Marshal Pétain and his Vichy regime. In Egypt and Palestine, General, later Field Marshal, Sir Maitland Wilson and French General Catroux looked anxiously at the Levant. Already German planes were coming in, and an Axis commission was running affairs. Despite the shortages of men and matériel, the Allies had to occupy the Levant.

But the Allies had to make sure that the Syrians and Lebanese would not side with the Vichy forces. That would render the task of the invading forces doubly difficult. Already it was a dangerous but essential venture.

So on June 8, as the Allied troops marched from Palestine into Syria and Lebanon, General Catroux, in the name of General de Gaulle, head of Free France, issued a proclamation to the Syrians and Lebanese. Thousands of pamphlets were dropped by plane. In them, Catroux said: "I come to put an end to the Mandate and to proclaim you free and independent. You will thus be henceforward free and independent states and will be able to constitute yourselves as distinct states or to amalgamate yourselves into a single state. Subject to those two hypotheses, your status of independence and sovereignty will be guaranteed by a treaty in which our mutual relations will be defined."

The Syrians and Lebanese cheered and awaited the victory of the Allies. After a short but tough fight, the Allied forces entered Beirut and Damascus, thus protecting the eastern approaches to the vital Suez Canal.

The inhabitants of the two countries sat and waited for their independence. On November 26, 1941, General Catroux again proclaimed to the Lebanese: "The Lebanese State will enjoy from now on the rights and prerogatives of an independent sovereign state. These rights and prerogatives are limited only by those restrictions which the present state of war and the safety of the country and of the Allied armies demands."

And because the war was still at their threshold, the Lebanese refrained from asking too much. But in the meantime, political activity was increasing steadily in the country, with the nationalist forces preparing to win the coming general elections, which would give the nation its first post-war Chamber of Deputies and a new president.

In the past, France had always run the elections the way she pleased in Lebanon. Presidents and ministers, deputies and government officers—all had to be approved by the French high commissioner.

Now two foreign forces were at play in the country: the British and French, who had fought side by side, were fighting each other for political domination in Lebanon. Each backed a different group of Lebanese leaders. The presence of two rival foreign powers gave Lebanon what were probably the first relatively free general elections in her modern history. Neither side could "cook" the elections so long as the other was watching so closely. The French and British neutralized each other's influence.

On August 29, 1943, Sheikh Beshara el Khoury was chosen as president of Lebanon, and he picked Riad Bey Solh as his prime minister. President El Khoury defeated his lifetime rival, French-backed Emile Eddé, in the presidential race.

Because of the peculiar religious situation in Lebanon, whose population consists of practically every known Christian and Muslim sect, with a fair sprinkling of Druzes thrown in, the new government decided that henceforth all religious groups should be represented in the Chamber and in the Cabinet. Thus, for example, the president is always a Christian of the Catholic Maronite sect, the prime minister is a Moslem Sunni, the vice-premier is a Greek Orthodox, the Minister of Defence a Druze. Others must include a Shiite Moslem, a Greek Catholic, Armenians, and sometimes a Protestant. The president of the Chamber of Deputies is a Shiite Moslem.

The new Lebanon was determined to give a fair deal to all citizens, irrespective of their religious convictions, and this was a tough policy to pursue. In the past, foreign powers had always played one religious group against the other, believing that a policy of "divide and rule" was the wisest course to pursue.

Premier Solh immediately started paving the way for the final phase of Lebanese independence. He called his cabinet members together and made it clear to the French that with the approval of President El Khoury he was going to alter the constitution of Lebanon to strike out or amend any articles that made the power of the Lebanese government subject to the approval of the mandatory power, France.

The French authorities objected. They stated that General Catroux had said that any independence would be announced after the signing of a treaty between France and Lebanon. And anyway, they added, it was the League of Nations that had given France the mandate over Lebanon, and only through the League of nations, or a similar body, could Lebanon gain her final independence.

"That's a lot of quibbling," answered the Lebanese. "There is no League of Nations any more and we are not going to wait until the governments get around to forming another grouping of nations. You promised us independence immediately in 1941, and that means now."

Meanwhile Britain, which had guaranteed General Catroux's promises to the Syrians and Lebanese in 1941, openly sympathized with the Lebanese.

The British minister to the Levant at that time was Maj. Gen. Sir Edward Spears. He had previously been chief liaison officer with the French army. It was on his plane that General de Gaulle had escaped to London, and it was with his help that he had started the Free French movement; but somewhere along the line the two men had quarreled, and the erstwhile friends had become bitter foes.

In October 1943, I called on General Spears, the first of many such visits during the next few months. He quite frankly admitted that the situation in Lebanon was very tense and bluntly predicted that unless the French showed some sympathetic understanding of Lebanon's impatience, there would be bloodshed in the country. The Lebanese, he said, were determined to get their full independence.

He explained that the Lebanese were determined to amend any items of their constitution that limited the government's authority and empowered the French to interfere in the running of the country. General Spears' usually smiling face hardened when he said, "Britain has guaranteed Free France's promise to the Lebanese, and we are very concerned about the current crisis."

A few days later, I called on the office of Camille Chamoun, minister of interior and a young man who had long fought for the independence of his country. This handsome, pleasant man was, as usual, cheerful, but there were lines of anxiety behind his smile. He admitted that the situation was very serious but asserted that the Lebanese government was determined to get rid of French interference or domination once and for all.

Later that day, I paid a courtesy call on the president of Lebanon; it was the first time I had met the middle-aged, capable leader of this republic. Of more than average height, this blue-eyed, stout, balding man with the beaming face looked more like a benevolent Dutch uncle than the shrewd, tough fighter he was.

Like most Lebanese politicians, Sheikh Beshara had been a lawyer by profession before going into politics. He knew his country and his countrymen thoroughly. In such a small republic, it was not difficult to know most people, but not only did he know them, he was surprisingly well acquainted with their personal problems and pleasures.

The president, too, expressed his concern at France's attitude and his country's hunger for total independence. We talked at some length of the situation and the problems facing the young Lebanese government.

The early days of November saw a lot of political fireworks. French High Commissioner Jean Helleu flew to Algiers to consult General de Gaulle and the French Committee of National Liberation. On November 8, the Lebanese Chamber met and forty-eight deputies present passed certain amendments to the constitution removing from it all clauses incompatible with their sovereignty and independence.

French Sureté agents that night visited all Lebanese newspaper offices and warned editors not to print the Chamber's decision. Two newspapers that did were indefinitely suspended.

Monsieur Helleu returned from Algiers on the ninth and asked the Lebanese government not to act hastily. But the die was cast.

On the evening of the tenth, General Spears had invited some members of the Lebanese government, Monsieur Helleu, and others to dinner in honor of King Peter of Yugoslavia, then visiting Beirut.

Among the guests was Selim Takla, then Lebanese foreign minister. The situation was very tense in town, and everybody was wondering what France would do. Helleu assured Spears that he would do nothing that might upset peace and order. A few hours later, he had arrested President El Khoury, Premier Solh, Foreign Minister Takla, Interior's Chamoun, and Minister of Justice Adel Osseiran. For good measure, he also captured Abdul Hamid Karameh, Muslim mufti of Tripoli and a popular politician over and above his religious function, and Pierre Gemayel, the youthful, dynamic leader of the paramilitary Christian organization, the Phalangists. The big adventure started then and produced a chain reaction that led to the first glimpse of Arab unity and a series of explosive events that were to rock the Middle East and have worldwide repercussions.

II
November 11, 1943

The telephone rang in my office in Cairo very early in the morning.

"This is Steve, Sam. Come down to my office. I've got an important communiqué for you."

"Steve" was Lt. Col. "Ned" Stephens, chief military press censor. I rushed down, grabbing hold of a mimeographed announcement. It was short—the French high commissioner in the Levant had ordered the arrest of the president of the Lebanese Republic and several of his cabinet. Hell was about to break loose in Beirut.

Within a couple of hours, a Royal Air Force plane was taking four correspondents to Beirut. The British had decided that they objected to France's high-handed attitude against the Lebanese and were aiding foreign correspondents to reach Lebanon by military transport, as all civilian traffic had been barred. It was obvious that they wanted to discredit France in the eyes of the world.

We landed at the tricky Beirut airfield with a British army conducting officer, ignored the silent but furious French Sureté officers, and went straight to the British legation. We drove in a British military car flying the Union Jack, and our English and American war correspondents' uniforms raised cheers from the few people to be seen in the empty, menacing streets. At strategic corners of the city, French steel-helmeted police and Senegalese troops, armed to the teeth, stood near machine-gun posts or tanks.

As we continued our silent way, we noticed here and there an overturned French truck or a charred French army car. Most of the big thoroughfares were clear of people. Once in a while the rattle of a machine gun would shatter the silence and echo through the nearby valleys.

Geoffrey Hoare, then with the *London Times*, Clare Hollingworth, a well-known British correspondent, Sonia Tomara from the *New York Herald Tribune*, and myself (then working for the United Press of America) were the first correspondents to reach Lebanon. Our conducting officer took us through the narrow, winding streets until we reached the British legation where General Spears was expecting us.

Curtly, he explained the situation. All four of us had been in Lebanon just a few weeks previously, and that was why we had been given priority in military transport. Just a few minutes were sufficient to bring our information up to date.

General Spears outlined the discussion he had had with French High Commissioner Helleu the night before, when the Frenchman had assured him that he would take no action likely to disturb public order. He told us that Christian and Muslim religious leaders had called on him and demanded British protection and aid against this high-handed French action. General Spears emphasized that the Christian religious leaders, normally extremely pro-French, had been among the first to protest against France's action.

This was the beginning of a unity that Lebanon had never seen before. While, previously, the country had been divided into two distinct religious groups, French action had, for the first time, united them together. Before the day was over, there were to be many more signs that a common front had been formed.

Thanks to my war correspondent's uniform, I was able to tour the city without interference from the French authorities. French patrols were everywhere. As I approached the Place de l'Étoile, where the Lebanese Chamber of Deputies was located,

I found Senegalese troops hitting passers-by with their rifle butts. A French officer stood by, nonchalantly smoking a cigarette. The people's only offence had been to come too near the chamber, where six of the fifty deputies had barricaded themselves.

I walked up to the offices of the United Press and found that two French officers were on the balcony, manning a machine gun, which covered Parliament Square. A short walk to the censorship, and I was informed that no stories about the events of the day would be passed by the French censor. Every cable was examined by three censors—British, French, and Lebanese.

The British, however, were very anxious for the story to get world-wide publicity. They had guaranteed the French promise that Lebanon was to have immediate independence. The eyes of the whole Arab world, which Britain was interested in keeping happy at the moment, were watching Britain's reaction to this affair.

It was not long, too, before we discovered that there was more than righteous indignation on the part of Britain. Here was a beautiful chance to get the French out of their firmest stronghold in the Middle East. In the future, it would be so much safer for Britain not to have a weakened, unpopular France as a partner in the Arab world. This time, the British had been lucky that, although the French in the Levant had backed Pétain, they were not able to resist the small Allied forces sent against them.

The next war might see Britain fighting Russia. There was no guarantee that France would not come out of the Second World War a communist state, and it would be much better to have her out of the way in the strategically important Levant. This was the thinking of many Englishmen at that time.

There were some, too, who whispered that General Spears was out to teach de Gaulle a lesson for having crossed him. Certainly, it was evident that the British minister had no time for de Gaulle and his free French—which he had helped create—any more. (De Gaulle lived to become one of the greatest men of the twentieth century, and General Spears became a small footnote in Middle Eastern history.)

And because the British wanted to get our stories out, we got them out. On that first day of November 11, a British military telephone connected us with our offices in Cairo, and we were each granted enough time to dictate an initial story of some two hundred words. From that day until the day the crisis ended, a British RAF plane came daily from Cairo and took our copy back to Cairo for British censorship, and thence to London and New York by cable. French censorship was thus by-passed.

That first night, presumably because General Spears was not sure that further action might develop after dark, he asked each one of the correspondents to spend the night at the house of one of the senior Lebanese employees at the British legation. He apparently feared the French might come to arrest them and hoped our presence would make them change their minds.

All day on the eleventh, and the following day, crowds of Lebanese citizens marched before the British and American legations demanding Anglo-American intervention against the French. Committees went up to see General Spears and U.S. Minister George Wadsworth.

"Unless the United States and Britain force the French to release our leaders, there will be a revolution throughout Lebanon and there will be repercussions throughout the Arab world," stated one committeeman. They invoked the Atlantic Charter.

One of the most impressive sights was to see a mass of women marching, arms locked together, through the streets, chanting for the liberation of their husbands and leaders. This was the first time the Muslim ladies had ever actively paraded in the Lebanon. There was Mrs. Solh, wife of the premier, and beside her, pretty blonde, blue-eyed Mrs. Chamoun. Perplexed French soldiers tried to disperse them without using force, but it was no use.

But although the British were sympathetic, they told the Lebanese they would not tolerate any nationwide action by them that might in any way affect the war effort. General Spears warned the Lebanese not to blow up roads or bridges that were vital to the British lines of communications, otherwise the British would have to fight the Lebanese. He said he was "shocked" at the French, and promised British intervention "soon."

Helleu had, in the meantime, appointed President Khoury's presidential rival as the provisional chief of state. Emile Eddé told the Lebanese he was working for the highest interests of Lebanon and urged the population to remain calm. Those who violated the law would be severely punished, he warned.

And while a state of confusion reigned in Beirut, the two Lebanese ministers who had escaped arrest had reached the safety of the hills and had rallied around them a few armed men. Vice-Premier Habib Abi Shahla and Druze Minister of Defence Emir Majid Arslan formed an "independent Lebanese government" to carry on the work.

The next day there was some fighting in Beirut's Muslim quarter where both Christians and Muslims had barricaded themselves in the very narrow streets. The French posted tanks at the entrances to the Basta quarter and fired at anyone showing his head.

There were still peaceful demonstrations marching before the Anglo-American legations. I was walking from my hotel to the Spears's mission and reached the street leading up to the British legation to find a mass of students, mainly from the American University of Beirut, standing in front of the barbed wire girdling Spears's buildings. Steel-helmeted British Tommies stood impassively guarding the entrances as the students demanded British intervention. At that moment, two truckloads of French and Senegalese troops drove up the other end of the street. Black and white soldiers jumped down and started firing at the students. A couple of youths fell, then some more, while one with blood streaming from his thigh hopped painfully past me.

It was then the British sentries lost their impassive objectivity and raised their rifles. Only a frenzied, shouted order from one of their officers prevented an Anglo-French fracas at that moment. But other British officers, watching from the legation windows, lost enough British phlegm to shout, "Bastards, salauds," at the Frenchmen. Others dashed down and carried the wounded Lebanese kids into the legation for first aid.

Developments quickly followed each other during the next few days. Winston Churchill ordered Australian-born Sir Richard Casey, British minister of state to the Middle East, to go to Beirut and stop this "nonsense." From Algiers, General de Gaulle announced that he was sending General Catroux to Cairo and Beirut to discuss matters and mediate.

From Cairo and Baghdad came reports that the Egyptian and Iraqi governments would break diplomatic relations with France, and there were many mass demonstrations against the French. It was the first tangible sign of post-war Arab unity.

Also in Algiers, where the harassed French Committee of National Liberation saw that matters were not turning out as they had expected, the blame was put on High Commissioner Helleu. The French were mystified. In the past, similar action would have had only the slightest echoes abroad. Now the whole world was looking towards Lebanon. For the first time people were interested in what happened in the Middle East.

Perhaps the subtle British propaganda machine, or the fact that people were genuinely starting to notice there were actually human beings living in that area, or a combination of both these factors had something to do with it. Then, too, there were many more correspondents floating around that area than ever before.

During all that time, I had seen the busy General Spears several times and naturally met several Lebanese. Some of the correspondents and I had even been taken to a secret session of the Lebanese deputies, held at the house of Sami bey Solh, cousin of Riad Bey. I felt it was time I met some of the French politicians. My previous attempts had failed, but this time a couple of us were conducted into the offices of High Commissioner Helleu.

Jean Helleu was a tall, gaunt man with red-rimmed eyes. People said he was fond of wine and women. He certainly was excitable. He had obviously been drinking.

"De Gaulle and the French Committe of National Liberation are in full agreement with the measures taken in Lebanon," he stated. This was his answer to Algiers for trying to make him the scapegoat: "Surely you do not think I would have taken such drastic action without the full consent of the committee, which is collectively responsible for all decisions," he protested.

Helleu revealed that when the committee in Algiers had reached the decision to arrest the president and his cabinet, he had warned them to expect trouble, but General de Gaulle ordered him to carry out his instructions. He told us that he had told the Lebanese government that France was anxious to grant Lebanon her independence, but that this step was not possible during wartime. He told the Lebanese, he said, that the French would not do more than carry on "most discreetly" with the mandate till the end of the war.

"I had liberal directives, but orders to arrest the Lebanese if they refused them."

Meanwhile "Dick" Casey, the British minister of state for the Middle East, was busy in Beirut. He told correspondents French action was a deed of "abysmal foolishness." He revealed that both the British and Free French had for long realized Lebanese impatience at not getting their independence. Mr. Winston Churchill and Foreign Secretary Anthony Eden in London had talked the matter over several times with General de Gaulle. He, Casey, had discussed it with Catroux. Spears in Beirut had been hobnobbing with Helleu. All these talks had resulted in the first free elections in Lebanon.

''We had long pleaded for a more liberal policy,'' Casey said, ''but our pleas fell on deaf ears. We British did definitely and positively underwrite the French pledge of independence to Syria and Lebanon.''

Casey revealed he had expected the Syrians, and not the Lebanese, to start the trouble in the Levant. Pressed by correspondents on Britain's motives in opposing the French, Casey retorted, ''We rate very highly the pledge as coguarantors made publicly before the world. We have no ulterior motive in Lebanon.''

Answering another question about the general British policy in the Middle East, Casey replied, ''We want a politically and economically contented Arab world.

''We did not encourage the Lebanese to bring pressure to bear on the French,'' he asserted. ''I believe had it not been for our calming influence, there would have been a bloody revolt.''

III
Guerilla Mountain Headquarters

While political palavers were taking place between American, British, and French generals and diplomats in Beirut, Cairo, Algiers, and London, more and more Lebanese were rallying around the two ministers still at liberty in the rugged hills.

For some time now the correspondents had been trying to reach their mountain hideout to which hundreds of armed Lebanese youths had been flocking to prepare for a fight. We knew that the place was not very far from Beirut, but with nobody willing to guide us there, it was difficult to venture out alone with both trigger-happy Frenchmen and Lebanese waiting to snipe at all suspicious-looking characters.

One day, however, while I was working on a story in my room at the Hotel Normandie, Naim Moghabghab, a young man I had known well in more peaceful days, strode into my room. He was armed to the teeth. Four grenades hung around his waist, and a huge revolver was strapped to his side.

"They tell me you want to visit our mountain headquarters," he stated. "If you are willing to start right away, I can take you there." I agreed to start right away. He collected a couple more correspondents, and we went out of the Normandie and got into an ancient car waiting for our guide.

We chugged along one of the main highways leading out of Beirut to the charming little hill station of Aley, fifteen kilometers away and three thousand feet above sea level. There was little movement on the roads and we passed through deserted villages, continued through Aley and on the Souk el Gharb road. On the way I saw a French armored car and motorcycles with machine guns mounted, keeping watch from various strategic points.

As we passed near the French outposts, our guide nonchalantly hummed Arab songs and quietly told the driver in Arabic, "If the French challenge us, step on the gas."

Fortunately, I was the only correspondent who understood, and I did not trouble to interpret this disquieting statement to my colleagues. Naim would have been summarily shot if caught with his private arsenal, and we would have had a lot of explaining to do. But the French patrols kept away from us, although they scanned our car with their binoculars.

Probably the sight of Allied uniforms discouraged them from stopping us.

As we rounded a sharp corner, we swung off the highway and onto a small rough track which led down the steep hillside. We turned one hairpin bend after another, until the driver jammed his brakes a few inches away from an avalanche of boulders which blocked further progress.

A group of tribesmen and armed Lebanese citizens appeared from nowhere and wanted to know what we were doing here. Our guide gave the Arab greeting, "Allah maakum" (God be with you), and told the sentries that we were the guests of Emir Majid, their commander. They recognized Naim and quickly dispersed once more to their camouflaged positions.

We left the car there and walked by several guerilla outposts where warriors were stationed in the dense olive groves of the region. Others were hidden in the terraced vineyards, and more were huddled in the pine forests and among the grey volcanic rocks. Whenever an overly suspicious fighter turned his gun in our direction, the guide would call out a greeting and identify the party.

Some, more friendly than others, came forward to shake our

hands. A few, with a nice sense of the dramatic, raised their rifles and scimitars in silent salute as we passed. A few snipers had chosen vantage points at the tops of pine trees.

It was a motley crew gathered there to do or die for Lebanon. There were the baggy Lebanese Druze tribesmen and the ragged toughs of the Beirut slums, the hardy mountaineers sporting riding breeches and boots, and the society boys who were dressed as if this was a duck shooting party.

Like most Lebanese youths, they could all handle a rifle quite efficiently, but they had no military training whatsoever. Some had had previous experience in street fighting or the occasional vendettas that break out among the clannish hillsmen. Others had previously fought each other in Christian-Muslim fights, but today they were standing side by side to meet a common foe.

Our party finally reached the commander's headquarters where we were greeted by the towering Emir Majid Arslan, clad in riding breeches and boots, a khaki sweater, and a white Bedouin kuffieh dotted with gold stars covering his head, held by a black camel hair "egal" or ring. This mustachioed Druze mountain prince was the scion of an old warrior family and minister of defence in the Lebanese government. It was around him that the Druze had gathered in his area of Bchamoun, a Druze stronghold in the hills overlooking Beirut. To them had flocked Christian and Muslim Lebanese, prepared to fight the French. Emir Majid carried a tommy gun, two bandoliers of bullets and a revolver strapped to his ample waist.

He greeted us standing in front of his "headquarters"—a peasant's house—one booted foot resting on a grey volcanic rock. Beside him stood his Druze bodyguards, all carrying machine guns and grenades.

After the customary exchange of courtesies, Emir Majid told us that he and his followers were determined not to return to their homes before the French government had released the imprisoned president and cabinet members. His force, he said, was steadily growing and the men were impatient. They wanted to start fighting the French, but he was awaiting the outcome of the talks between the French representatives and the Anglo-American diplomats whose main concern was to prevent an all-out revolt that could only hamper the Allied war effort.

The emir admitted, "My army is not disciplined, but they understand my orders." The whole thing seemed unreal, and I could not help feeling it was something out of a comic opera, with the ancient and modern contrasting strangely in the lovely setting of the Lebanese mountainside, overlooking a strangely calm and wonderfully blue Mediterranean.

This was the first of several visits I made to Bchamoun, seat of the Lebanese guerillas. In subsequent trips I met Vice-Premier Habib Abi Shahla, that cigar-smoking shrewd politician with a delightful sense of humour. He never lost his cheerful attitude on life throughout his enforced stay in this village. This rumpled man, normally one of the best-dressed in Beirut society, kept the administrative machine going.

It was at this mountain hideout that the Lebanese hoisted the new flag of their country. Previously the national emblem had been the French tri-color with a Lebanese cedar tree in the middle. They now chose a red, white, and red flag with the cedar in the middle as their flag and, as they thundered their national anthem, raised the new flag of free Lebanon over their mountain stronghold.

There were a few clashes with French patrols in the region, but at no time did the Lebanese stage any offensive operation against the French. Emir Majid had sworn that he could drive them into the sea. He said, quite truthfully, that other forces had concentrated in other mountain areas and waited for his orders. Whether or not he could have driven the French into the sea, I cannot say. Certainly, had his forces swung into action, there would have been much bloodshed and damage done to both sides.

But outside of a few unimportant and minor skirmishes, the Lebanese forces in the mountains remained quiet, although their growing strength was a mounting threat that the Anglo-American and French politicians, gathered in Beirut, had to take into serious consideration as they thrashed out the problem and sought a solution.

George Wadsworth spoke for the United States. America had recognized the independence of Lebanon and wanted to avoid further trouble in that area. General Spears represented Britain and he was joined by Sir Richard Casey, then British minister of state. Both men saw a great deal of Lebanese leaders, sent emissaries to discuss matters with the ''Bchamoun government'' and at the same time talked with General Catroux who had in the meantime arrived from Algiers and was handling matters. Jean Helleu was a man of the past.

IV
Conferences in Beirut

During those hectic days, conferences succeeded each other, as Allied politicians, not so allied over their Lebanese policies, met and discussed matters. Lebanese religious leaders, both Christian and Muslim, hustled back and forth between the various legations, submitting protests, demands, and prayers.

General Catroux, the soldier-diplomat of Free France, was now handling the unenviable task of trying to seek a formula which would not oust the French from Lebanon. His first task was to meet the various Lebanese religious leaders and reach an armed truce between the French authorities and the Beirut population until the outcome of his talks was known.

The 6:30 P.M. curfew was extended by the French to 8:30 P.M. The telephone system, which had closed down, was reopened. A few shops had lifted their shutters, but on the whole the general strike went on in Beirut.

The war of words continued. Lebanese patriots distributed pamphlets urging the population to stand fast. All papers had been closed, but a clandestine paper was avidly read by all. The French had started printing a paper "De quoi s'agit-il?" trying to explain their viewpoint.

The French-controlled radio station openly criticized the British for their attitude and blamed them for the situation. British-controlled radio stations in various parts of the Middle East continued to blast the French.

Russia also put in its word. Through the Lebanese Communist party, the Kremlin hit at the French and gained further sympathy in Lebanon. The communists demanded the release of all detained persons, the reestablishment of constitutional life, abrogation of all decrees since the suspension of the constitution, and the expulsion of all French "fascist" elements in the Levant.

These were the first words uttered by the communists in the Levant. The Reds were comparative newcomers into that area. They were to grow up very quickly.

Britain's Casey arrived in Beirut from Cairo to meet Catroux and told the press that he hoped to shortly reach a solution acceptable to both the French and the Lebanese, which would both safeguard French interests and Lebanese independence.

Casey and Catroux had their first meeting, and after that Casey announced, "I cannot truthfully say that the tension in Lebanon has relaxed. The serious situation still exists in the country."

That was understandable. Catroux had already seen a few foreign correspondents and told them what he thought of "British intervention" in this strictly "Franco-Lebanese affair." Catroux met us in the sumptuous house placed at his disposal by the French authorities in Beirut's fashionable Sursock quarter. This olive-skinned, thin diplomat could hardly hide his impotent fury at the British as he talked for forty-five minutes to French, British, and American correspondents.

He presented the French case in no mean terms when he demanded, through the press, that Britain should cease interfering "in what is a purely Franco-Lebanese affair." He reaffirmed France's unwillingness to give up the mandate until the end of the war and the signing of a treaty guaranteeing France's interests in the Levant. He asserted that the Lebanese were wrong in presuming that his 1941 declaration meant the immediate freedom of the country. The independence was to be preceded by a treaty, he insisted.

Why should Britain have insisted on a treaty with Iraq before giving that country a fair measure of independence, he asked bitterly. He also compared the French administrative responsibilities to those of the British in Palestine. Both powers held the mandates. "I wonder how much the British would like to interfere with their running of Palestine?" he stated.

Catroux said he hoped that he would soon reach a solution "based on mutual concessions." He announced he was studying every angle of the problems and was meeting various Lebanese leaders. "I am a man of goodwill. I made the declaration of independence and reestablished constitutional life in Lebanon. I want to give the maximum independence to Lebanon and also want French interests safeguarded," he concluded.

He appealed to the British to concentrate on military matters in Lebanon and leave the political problems to the French. He warned that if the local population saw that the two powers were at loggerheads, they would exploit the situation further. But his plea was unheard. Britain continued to press the matter and back the Lebanese. They had interests throughout the Arab world. Egypt and Iraq were watching Britain's attitude in Lebanon.

The British tried to handle the matter in such a way as not to completely alienate France. After all, both were still fighting a global war. But France was weakened, and the potential importance of the Middle East outweighed French sensitivities.

After more talks, the French finally announced that they would release all the Lebanese leaders interned at Rashayya fortress. Lebanon would gradually take over administrative matters and at the end of the war, the country would be rid of foreign troops. The matter took two years to be finally settled, with the problem coming before the Security Council and the United Nations Assembly, and another Franco-Levantine clash. But the second time, the scene was in Syria and the date—1945.

In the meantime, President El Khoury and his imprisoned government returned in triumph to Beirut, the "Bchamoun heroes" marched into the capital, Britain was hailed as the friend of the Arabs, and France started planning her comeback.

A measure of freedom had come, but more headaches and trials lay ahead.

V
The Arab League—1944

In 1944, by the grace of God and the encouragement of Great Britain, the League of Arab States was born. It consisted of seven countries—Egypt, Syria, Lebanon, Iraq, Saudi Arabia, Transjordan, and Yemen.

They did not all like each other, but they realised that it might be a good idea to get together and cooperate on problems of common interest. Besides, the British government, which at that time wielded great influence in these countries, favoured the idea. Foreign Secretary Anthony Eden had given the green light in the House of Commons.

So setting aside their differences, they concentrated on the matters in which they were all vitally interested—mainly the problem of keeping Palestine Arab. They signed the Protocol of Alexandria in October 1944, in which they agreed not to trespass on each other's frontiers, to aid one another in times of stress, and to work for the common good of the Arab world. The League came into actual being in March 1945.

They established a general headquarters in Cairo and set up a secretariat with a secretary-general at its head. The delegates of the seven countries chose a veteran fighter for Arab freedom for this post, Abdel Rahman Azzam Bey, later to become a pasha, and one of the most respected and persevering champions of the Arab world.

Abdel Rahman Azzam, a lean, tough man in his middle fifties, had fought in lost causes from the Balkans to Libya.

As soon as he had assumed this job, Azzam started organising his cherished Arab League. He prepared the general sessions which were held every six months, or whenever the situation warranted a meeting of the leaders of the Arab states. He also formed committees to coordinate culture, health programs, agriculture, and all other matters which might be better handled by the Arab world as a whole, rather than by states working singly.

Born in Cairo in 1891, Azzam began his education in the Egyptian capital and later went to England where he graduated at the London University. He started off as a medical student at St. Thomas Hospital, but gave up studies, for which he had little inclination anyway, and volunteered in the Turkish army.

This was the start of his struggle for the Arab cause. He saw action for the first time in the Balkans, but soon left the collapsing Turks to continue the fight against the Italians in Libya in 1911. There, he rallied round him a comparatively large number of men and actively engaged in underground warfare. He scored a number of military successes and managed to be a thorn in the side of the Italians who had taken over Libya from the Turks.

He fought with the Libyans against Italian domination of this Arab country and as one of its commanding officers he declared the country a republic in 1918. The Allied victory put an end to his dream and the Italians were maintained in Libya.

He went back to Egypt and abandoned the sword for the pen. He contributed numerous articles on the Arab cause to local papers and continued to take a deep interest in the affairs of the Arab countries in general and of Libya in particular. He also extended all possible help to those Libyan chiefs who had sought refuge in Egypt from Italian colonial rule. He joined Saad Zaghloul, champion of Egyptian nationalism, in 1924.

Then followed a relatively quiet and uneventful period until 1936 when Azzam Bey, as he then was, entered the Egyptian Ministry of Foreign Affairs and was appointed minister to Iran, Iraq, Afghanistan, and Saudi Arabia. He held this position for three years and started his friendship with King Ibn Saud—a friendship which was to bear fruit when the Arab League was formed. Azzam was then transferred as Minister to Turkey and Bulgaria. He resigned during the same year and went to London to participate in the conference on the Palestine problem which, like other Arab problems, was of vital concern to this Arab leader.

When war broke out, Azzam was placed at the head of the Egyptian Territorial Army. His work gave him no scope to do the things he liked, and he could accomplish little for the Arab cause. Later, he became Minister of Social Affairs.

In 1944, Anthony Eden, then British foreign secretary, gave official British blessings for the formation of an Arab League. This was the opportunity that Azzam had been waiting for. He had since left the Ministry of Social Affairs and straightaway threw himself into this new British-sponsored plan. Britain had in the past opposed the idea of a body combining the Arab states. Now she gave her support. From her end the road was now clear, though jammed with hazards within the Arab states.

There were rivalries among the Arab rulers and leaders. They suspected one another of having designs on the caliphate, on one another's territories, and some did not want to get together with those they considered their traditional enemies. Saudi Arabia did not want to abandon her longtime isolationism. Neither did Yemen, and especially in any deal in which King Ibn Saud had a hand. The Hashemites ruling Iraq and Transjordan hated Ibn Saud. The Syrians and Lebanese suspected the Transjordan monarch of wanting to use such an organisation to put through his cherished dream of a Greater Syria, comprising Palestine, Syria, Lebanon, and Transjordan under his rule. The Christians in Lebanon thought such a league would become a Muslim union to the detriment of Christian interests. Others suspected that King Farouk would use the league to further his own ends and believed he wanted to become the new caliph.

With tremendous patience and masterful diplomacy, Abdel Rahman Azzam talked first to one group and then to the other. Slowly he got people round to the idea. He flew to Saudi Arabia, to Baghdad, Beirut, and Damascus.

"Give this league a chance," he pleaded. "If it fails you, then you can drop it. Put aside your suspicions."

To help him in his work, the Egyptian government had appointed him minister plenipotentiary in charge of Arab Affairs.

So well and so hard did he argue that he succeeded in dispelling most suspicions. In the end, the various countries agreed on the league's statutes which were signed in Cairo in March 1945. Azzam Pasha could well be proud of his achievement and the charter of the Arab League was almost entirely due to his efforts.

It was no surprise when he was elected the first secretary-general of the league. There is no doubt that Azzam was the soul of the Arab League. During the first years of its existence, he added greatly to his political stature and the league's reputation. Both within the Arab world and in international sessions he won acclaim as a subtle, broad-minded diplomat. By his able guidance, the league which had started under the accusation of being a "British pawn" developed a personality and strength of its own.

The story is told of a conversation Azzam had in Beirut with a Russian diplomat. The Soviet was trying to force Azzam into admitting that the Arab League was a tool of British diplomacy.

"You must admit, Pasha, that the Arab League is a British product."

Azzam glanced at the Russian and, fingering the lapel of his tweed coat, answered, "This coat is also a British product, but it keeps me warm." He does not deny that it was with British support that the league started, but once it had been brought into being, he claimed that its sole purpose was to safeguard and further Arab interests.

The greater part of the league's work dealt with the grave political problems of the Arab world. From the beginning, the leaders swore they would do everything in their power to keep Palestine an Arab country. They also rose against France in 1945 when the French shelled Damascus and other Syrian towns. When the United Nations got together, the Arab states formed a strong bloc, coordinating their views on all major issues.

It soon became evident that the league which started off as a British-sponsored project was growing to be an independent body that liked to think and act for itself. So much so that there were times when the British were suspected of trying to sabotage the league they helped to form. In several cases, the Arab League states opposed Britain at the United Nations.

It was not all smooth sailing, however. As in any other bloc, the various members had their quarrels. In the Arab League, some of these differences and enmities dated back several generations. There was, for example, the dispute between King Abdul Aziz Ibn Saud of Saudi Arabia and King Abdullah of Transjordan. King Abdullah's father, the Sherif Hussein, had been pushed out of Arabia by the then desert chieftain, Ibn Saud, after a long and bitter war in the merciless sands. Abdullah, who had commanded one of his father's armies, could not forget that defeat.

When the British and French carved up the Middle East between them after World War I, he was given the emirate of Transjordan under British mandate. His brother Feisal was given the kingdom of Iraq. The Hashemites, as the family of Sherif Hussein was known, still harboured a grudge against Ibn Saud.

Transjordan, Iraq, and Saudi Arabia had become members of the Arab League, but their leaders still scowled at each other across the conference tables. There were some embarassing incidents between the delegates, and the teamwork was somewhat marred by the bitter memories of former opponents.

This unspoken but obvious bitterness continued until King Farouk of Egypt stepped in and organised the conference of Inchass.

He got together the heads of all the Arab states, kings and presidents, and convinced them to smoke the pipe of peace. They buried the hatchet and made up. King Ibn Saud was not present, but his eldest son and heir, Prince Saud, was there to embrace King Abdullah. From that day, the tension at the Arab League meetings eased considerably. If the kings had made their peace, their followers were more than ready to sit comfortably together. But this honeymoon did not last long.

There were other differences, and such differences will continue, as in any other group of nations trying to work together. But they were all willing to unite on matters of common interest. There was some progress in coordinating educational, economic, and other problems throughout the Arab world. This work was difficult because some of the Arab countries were more advanced than others. Saudi Arabia, Transjordan, and Yemen had not yet achieved the progress of Egypt, Iraq, Syria, and Lebanon. In turn, the latter group was also at different points in standards of living. As the league tackled problems affecting all these states, every individual nation was simultaneously working on its own to put through local programs of social reform, industrialization of various areas, modernisation of agriculture, and the general raising of standards of living. These problems were handled in different ways by the different countries, depending on the resources at their disposal.

In the political field, the Arab League had always followed a program which fitted the framework of the United Nations. The league had pressed for a peaceful solution of all problems concerning the Arab states and had consistently opposed the use of violence as a means of settlement. Notable exception was the disastrous Palestine campaign.

The moral force of the league began playing a role in the various crises of the Arab world and contributed to solving most problems. The Syrian trouble with France saw the league actively support Syria, and the weight of this support told on the French.

In order to strengthen ties with the Arab world, Britain forced France out of Syria and Lebanon.

When Egypt took its dispute with Britain before the Security Council, the Arab states all stood behind Egypt and maintained that the matter was as vital to them as for Egypt itself.

The moral strength of the league and the coordinated work of the Arab states at first greatly aided the Palestine Arabs in their fight against Zionism. There is no doubt that the attitude of the Arab League and its stiff opposition to a Jewish Palestine was instrumental in preventing even greater Anglo-American support of the Zionists. When finally the Palestine problem was turned over to the United Nations, the Arab League again exerted every effort to put over the Arab viewpoint. This effort carried far more weight than anything the Palestine Arabs could have done alone. However, it was not enough to carry through against Zionist political know-how and influence.

The Arab League later took up the cudgels for another explosive Arab cause—North Africa. The three countries which form what is commonly known as French North Africa are Morocco, Tunisia, and Algeria. For years, nationalist movements had existed in these countries, working and fighting to get rid of the Spanish and French forces of occupation in Morocco and French rule in Tunisia and Algeria. With the exception of the Riff war waged by Emir Abdel Krim, the other campaigns had roused little or no world concern. Thousands of North Africans were bombed and killed in 1943 without anybody getting excited about it. In contrast, the minor skirmishes in Lebanon around the same time attracted worldwide attention.

Nothing was done to excite mass interest in North Africa until the Arab League, and specifically Abdel Rahman Azzam, began campaigning for these countries' independence and exposing the situation behind the French "iron curtain." His approach to the problem caught public attention in the United

States where, without neglecting his work in favor of the Egyptian and Palestinian causes, Azzam succeeded in North Africa as well.

Azzam had also aided exiled and other North African nationalists to set up headquarters in Cairo and cooperate with the Arab League. They continued to press their plea in favor of independence. This North African office also sent various members campaigning through the Middle East and the United States. The statutes of the Arab League prevent the admission of Arab nations that had not yet attained sovereignty as fully pledged members, but the league worked in close cooperation with both the Palestinian Arab political leaders and the North African bureau.

Many people have wondered whether the Arab League was really a Muslim League working for the benefit of Muslims everywhere. The Arab League is essentially Arab, and while the majority of the member states and delegates are Muslims, there are Christian Arabs among them. There is no question of the Arabs admitting non-Arab Muslims into the league. The whole program is based on the requirements of the Arab world, bound together by ties of race, language and geographic affinities. The Arab world, predominantly Muslim, may and does work closely with Muslim non-Arab states, but the purpose of the league remains Arab first and foremost.

The leaders of the Arab League have constantly emphasized this point. Turkey, Iran, and other Muslim states might have liked at one time to be members of this league, but the Arab states preferred to remain an entity based on race rather than religion. Individual states within the Arab League are, however, at liberty to establish close ties with other Muslim non-Arab nations.

But despite their united front on many problems, the Arab League states were not as united over other issues as they could have been. True, the leaders had smoked the pipe of peace at

King Farouk's Inchass palace, but they had not completely abandoned whatever conflicting pet schemes they had dreamed up over the years. So that while they started off well, they did not pull together when the real test came along. That test was Palestine.

There had been many vain boasts made which the league never fulfilled. Many words had been spoken which were subsequently proven to be just idle, meaningless platitudes. When the day of reckoning came, when the league had to undergo its baptism of fire, the underlying disputes, which had never been settled, boiled over and caused them to suffer both political setbacks and military defeats.

These disputes were both inter-Arab and international. One of the unfortunate traits of the Arabs, born mainly because of a courtesy that borders on hypocrisy, is to avoid directly tackling any embarrassing situation. So that when two Arab leaders disagreed on some matter, both felt much relieved by delicately skirting the problem and agreeing to leave the solution to time, rather than to frankly discuss the matter and get it over with.

It had been argued that the league would have died an early death had it been forced to tackle these problems in its infancy. After the tragic events in Palestine, which almost killed the league, many who advocated this policy regretted it and wished that the various problems between the Arab states had been tackled bluntly at the beginning, regardless of whose sensibilities would have been hurt.

What were those conflicting aims, the pet schemes and projects that created rivalry? What matters did they delicately skirt rather than tackle bluntly? They were not many, but they were deep-rooted, born in other generations and handed down as a bitter heritage of the days when a desperate Britain showered promises right and left to rival forces in the Middle East.

VI
Greater Syria

King Abdullah of Transjordan, that staunch ally of Britain, was at the same time a dreamer and a practical man. Paradoxical as that may sound, many who knew the ruler of this tiny Arab kingdom will confirm this description of the colorful desert monarch.

He was one of the sons of Sherif Hussein, who ruled over the deserts of what is now Saudi Arabia. Long before King Ibn Saud was anything but the chieftain of a fierce tribe in the heart of the Arabian peninsula, the Hashemite dynasty ruled the Hedjaz in style. Sherif Hussein held the Muslim holy cities of Mecca and Medina and claimed descendance from the Prophet Mohammed.

Up to 1916, the Sherif owed allegiance to the Turkish Sultan in Constantinople, but under the influence of his four sons, Abdullah, Faisal, Ali, and Zaid, he became interested in the Arab struggle for independence. At that time the British government, seeking allies in her fight against Germany and Turkey, promised Sherif Hussein the independence of all Arab territories under Turkish rule. There was a certain amount of vagueness in these promises, contained in an exchange of letters, eight in number, between Sir Henry McMahon, then British high commissioner in Egypt, and Sherif Hussein.

For example: "Subject to that modification, and without prejudice to the treaties concluded between us and certain Arab Chiefs." And: "As for the regions lying within the proposed frontiers, in which Great Britain is free to act without detriment to the interests of her ally, France, I am authorized to give you the following pledges on behalf of the Government of Great Britain and to reply as follows to your note: That, subject to the modifications stated above, Great Britain is prepared to recognize and uphold the independence of the Arabs in all the regions lying within the frontiers proposed by the Sherif of Mecca.''

This was the signal for the Arab revolt, the formation of the sherifian army which fought with General Allenby and defeated the Turks. The exploits of this force were romantically chronicled by T.E. Lawrence—Lawrence of Arabia.

Then came the conflicting British promises and secret agreements. First there was the Sykes-Picot Agreement, in which the British, Czarist Russians, and French agreed to divide the Arab world between them, and the Balfour Declaration, in which Britain promised ''a national home for the Jewish people'' in Palestine.

The secret Sykes-Picot Agreement was dramatically revealed when the Bolsheviks seized power in Russia and disclosed all czarist state secrets. The Turks passed the agreement through the lines to their Arab enemies in the hopes of turning them against the British. Then came the Basset Letter, sent on behalf of the British Government by Lt. Col. J. R. Basset, then acting British agent at Jeddah, reassuring the Arabs of Britain's goodwill: ''His Majesty's Government reaffirm their former pledge in regard to the liberation of the Arab peoples,'' the letter stated.

Sherif Hussein fought on beside the British against the Turks. Then came the ''great double cross'' when Britain and France divided the Arab world, established the mandate system by which France had the mandatory power in Syria and Lebanon, and Britain took over Palestine and Transjordan. Britain maintained her promise to the Jews despite the protests of the Sherif.

In 1924, King Ibn Saud, who had in the meantime conquered the whole of the Nejd plateau in the hinterland of the Arabian peninsula, pushed westwards towards the coast, defeated the Sherif's armies and occupied the whole of the peninsula.

The Sherif who had abdicated in favour of his son Ali, first went into exile and then died at the court of his son, Emir, later King Abdullah who had been given the emirate of Transjordan as a consolation prize by the British.

Ali fled to Baghdad, which was the capital of the British mandate of Iraq, with another of the Sherif's sons, Faisal, as ruler. Faisal had for a short time ruled as king of Syria until he was thrown out by the French in 1920.

During that short period between 1916 and 1922, the seeds of future conflicts and the enmities that were to shatter the Arab world were born. Under the mandatory powers, the Syrian and Lebanese republics developed nationalistic feelings quite apart from the old dream of one united kingdom grouping all the former Ottoman-dominated Arab areas.

In Palestine, Jewish immigration started and the British quelled three Arab revolts opposing this Zionist influx into the country. Palestinian Arab leaders rose and intrigued against each other, and against Arab leaders who showed an interest in Palestine.

King Ibn Saud planted his flag firmly over the Arabian peninsula and even tried to advance into Transjordan. He was thrown back by a merciless pounding dealt by the Royal Air Force, as Britain felt that it must back Abdullah.

And in Transjordan, King Abdullah remembered his father who had died a broken old man, grieved at the empty promises and lamenting the Arab kingdom of Greater Syria which was never formed. Never during his reign did Abdullah once abandon his Greater Syria plan—a plan which simply consists of uniting Syria, Lebanon, Palestine, and Transjordan into one united country under the rule of the Hashemites. A Hashemite king also ruled in Iraq, and together Greater Syria and Iraq would have formed a powerful bloc.

Early in his reign, King Abdullah decided the one sure way to realize his dream was to ally himself wholeheartedly to the British. He felt that Britain was the most Arab-minded of the great powers and threw his lot with it. He let bygones be bygones, forgot that the British had betrayed his father, and dreamed of the future. If his plans had any chance of success, it would be with British help. And on more than one occasion he came within an ace of realising his cherished dream.

While he continued to prepare his Greater Syria, he aroused the fury of other Arab leaders.

The Syrian republicans did not want it.

Neither did the Christian Lebanese. Nor were the Muslim Lebanese particularly happy about it.

The anti-British Haj Amin el Husseini, leader of Palestine Arabs, fought it tooth and nail.

The Zionists in Palestine plotted against it.

King Ibn Saud feared it might be the start of a Hashemite campaign against him.

And Egypt's King Farouk did not like it.

Each one had a different reason for opposing Abdullah's Greater Syria, but they were all united in opposing it. And when the Palestine issue came to a head with the departure of the British forces on May 14, 1948, the Arabs were still at loggerheads, although they publicly professed to be completely united.

Throughout the life of the Arab League, whenever the question of Greater Syria was broached, it would be diplomatically sidetracked. The charter of the Arab League guaranteed the existing frontiers of every Arab state. However, should any want to unite of their own free will, they could do so, said the charter.

King Abdullah told me time and time again: "Of course, the leaders in those states which should be in Greater Syria oppose me. They are anxious to maintain their seats of government. But the majority of the people are for a united Arab state, which would be strong enough to fight Zionism and form a powerful political and economic unit.''

In reply, the others stated: ''We are happy as we are. The Arab League is a sufficient bond between us.''

And once a leading Syrian statesman told me: ''Next time you see King Abdullah, ask him whether he would abdicate should the Arabs indicate they want to unite—but under a republican regime and not a monarchy.''

This then, was one of the main disputes which split the members of the Arab League. The Greater Syria plan met rigid opposition, too, from two powerful Arab nations not directly affected by it—Egypt and Saudi Arabia.

King Ibn Saud knew that the Transjordan ruler had not forgotten that the Hashemites had once ruled the Arab peninsula. He feared that once Greater Syria came into being, Abdullah and the Hashemite-ruled Iraq would join forces to reconquer Saudi Arabia. He firmly opposed any plan for Arab unity other than the united Arab League, loosely knit but with each nation maintaining its own frontiers.

In Egypt, the government decided that King Abdullah was too influenced by the British to be a fit ruler for a united Arab kingdom. Besides, Egypt was unchallenged as the leader of the Arab League states in its present form, and resented Abdullah's continued efforts to create a Greater Syria which would upset this leadership. It was inconceivable to Egyptian minds that this little kingdom of 400,000 should covet their position of the leading Arab state—they whose country numbered over twenty million with large cities, a flourishing economy, and well-organized economic and political life.

VII
The Fertile Crescent

Another of the stumbling blocks barring the way to Arab unity was the dispute created among the Arab leaders concerning the Fertile Crescent plan, that project so dear to the hearts of such Iraqi leaders as General Nuri es Said Pasha, veteran fighter for Arab freedom.

The Fertile Crescent is not much different from King Abdullah's Greater Syria project. It consists of the unification of Iraq, Syria, Lebanon, Transjordan, and Palestine, but it is an idea sponsored by Iraqi leaders rather than by Transjordan.

Men such as Nuri es Said Pasha, several-time premier of Iraq and one of the driving forces behind this scheme, believed that the unification could be achieved in several ways. It could start with the fusion of Iraq and her neighbour, Syria, at the request of the Syrian government. Nuri Pasha several times tried to convince various Syrian regimes of taking that step on the road to Arab unity. Regularly something would arise that would defeat the plan.

A united Syria and Iraq would then pave the way for the annexation of Lebanon, Syria's neighbour.

Transjordan would willingly join. The question of who of the Hashemite rulers should be the supreme ruler never seemed to present any difficulties, according to loyal Hashemite followers; although other neutral observers have always predicted that should such unification start, there was bound to be some jealous bickering among the rulers and their heirs for the paramount leadership of this area.

Palestine was naturally included in the Fertile Crescent scheme, although with the influx of Jews and their occupation of a major part of the Holy Land, nothing short of another war might have regained the former Arab lands into the fold.

There were many people in the various countries affected by the Fertile Crescent plan who were much in favor of this scheme, but there were as many who opposed it. And among those who in principle approved the idea, a considerable portion refused to cooperate with those leaders trying to put it through.

Of the many supporters of the Fertile Crescent scheme, two stood out very prominently. The first we have already mentioned, General Nuri es Said Pasha. The second was a well-known Palestinian Arab leader, Moussa el Alami.

Nuri Pasha, a veteran Iraqi leader, was since 1913 one of the champions of Arab unity and independence. He fought alongside Lawrence of Arabia and General Allenby. One of the Iraqis who invited Emir Feisal, son of Sherif Hussein of Mecca, to become King of Iraq, he was among the most loyal followers of the Hashemites and had always followed a decidedly pro-British policy. His British leanings twice caused him to flee Iraq when extreme nationalists staged anti-British uprisings.

This green-eyed shrewd politician had always favored a Fertile Crescent uniting the Arab countries east of Suez. The name "Fertile Crescent" had been given to this scheme because, on the map, that fertile part of the Arab world in Asia takes the shape of a crescent.

Moussa el Alami, a Palestinian Arab leader, a graduate of Trinity Hall, Cambridge, had also been a fervent supporter of Iraq as the most promising of the Arab states. This Palestinian barrister had always felt that the salvation of Palestine from Zionism and of the Arab states from their own lethargy lay in an Iraqi-led united nation.

There were others who favored this scheme, but not under the sponsorship of Nuri Pasha. "We might as well hand the Arab states to Britain on a platter," they said. "A Fertile Crescent under Nuri simply means that all these countries become puppets of Britain. We want a Fertile Crescent that is free to choose her own allies, and whose policies are not dictated by Whitehall."

There are others who did not want the Fertile Crescent scheme at all because it affected their own newly found ideas of nationalism, or because it merely clashed with their own interests. Just as they opposed the Greater Syria plan, Egypt and Saudi Arabia opposed the Fertile Crescent.

There was less opposition in Syria to the Fertile Crescent scheme than there was to King Abdullah's project, but there, too, many of the Syrians supported the idea only on condition that it would not be led by Nuri Pasha.

In Lebanon, most of the Christians opposed this and any other scheme aiming to unite them with other Arab states. They said that the peculiar situation of Lebanon, which is a Christian state with a large Muslim minority, makes acceptance of this idea impossible. The Christians have always had some kind of autonomy and have with their Muslim countrymen advanced much farther than the Arabs of neighboring countries. It would be difficult for them to join and be subjected to a leadership of people who have not reached their own standards of civilization, they allege. Some Christians favor a Fertile Crescent that would exclude Lebanon.

Many of the Lebanese Muslims, however, supported the unification of the Arab states and preferred to be led by a non-Lebanese than a Lebanese Christian. For nationalism in the Middle East is often tinged with religious feeling. Some of the younger ambitious elements among the Lebanese Muslims, however, felt that in a Greater Syria or a Fertile Crescent unity, they would be able to play a major role because they were more advanced than their fellow Arabs.

The Iraqi version of King Abdullah's Greater Syria is yet another heritage of the days of the Arab rebellion that promised much and gave little of freedom to the Arabs. In those days, Nuri es Said Pasha was a dashing young officer in the Arab army, a man who even previously had plotted to free his brethren from the Turkish yoke.

But because he was a fighter, he did not despair when Arab unity failed to materialize, as he had hoped, immediately after World War I. He realized that the Arab states were weak and that he must hitch his star to one of the powers, and like his Hashemite overlords, he decided on Britain as the one great nation interested enough and able to help achieve his goal.

He believed in his Iraq countrymen even when they stopped believing in him. He worked for an outlet to the Mediterranean and the fusion of those Arab states surrounding his country. Rightly or wrongly, he overrode all Iraqi extreme nationalist hatred for Britain and suppressed any anti-British move, and always stated that he did this in the interests of his country. Only through Britain's help, he is said to have told other Iraqi leaders, could Iraq ultimately achieve the unity of the Arab states.

But his faith in Britain had landed him in many a tight spot. Twice he was forced to flee an angry Iraq, which rose against him and Britain. Sincere Iraqi nationalists were used by Germans and Italians before and during World War II to fight Britain and her supporters in Baghdad, and after the war, the communists put in their agents. They, too, aroused the youth of the country against the pro-British policy of the Hashemites and their ministers.

"Arab unity is a wonderful thing," said the Russians, "but not if it must be achieved through Nuri es Said, and not if you must sign away your birthright to the British through some binding treaty." And the people rose on the eve of the signing of a "Portsmouth treaty" that would have bound England and Iraq closely together.

So, in the Fertile Crescent as in the Greater Syria plan, the battle went on between those who believed that, for the present anyway, the Arab League was a sufficient bond between them and those who wanted more. It was a fight between a newly created nationalism, based on frontiers created since World War I, and a wider concept of unity of those who did not recognize those man-made borders.

But there was, too, the struggle of the various leaders of the Arab world for the paramount leadership of this area. It was a jockeying of positions among kings and presidents. The Hashemites and their loyal followers could never forget that they were promised the Arab world for their own in 1916.

King Ibn Saud defeated the Hashemites in the Arabian peninsula and wanted no further change.

King Farouk stood for a status quo, too. A close friend of the Saudi Arabian monarch, the two rulers were in agreement that the countries should maintain their present frontiers. Egypt was not affected in any Arab unity plan, but the states in their present division looked to Farouk's Egypt as the unchallenged leader of the Arab world from North Africa to the borders of Turkey. The growth of Hashemites' influence would diminish the supremacy of Egypt.

In both Syria and Lebanon, republics had grown and flourished, despite continued unrest in Syria. It was not easy to expect that people in power would readily give up their seats to outsiders after having enjoyed the privileges of government—and without being too conscious of its duties.

VIII
Anglo-Arab Relations

The root of the trouble between the Arab states was that they had never had a coordinated foreign policy vis-à-vis Britain. For decades, the world power most interested in the Middle East generally, and the Arab world particularly, was Britain. History has shown that Britain had much to do with the course of events in these countries.

But as time went on the world changed. There was a new spirit which crept into the minds of those Arab countries who for long had been dominated and led by one foreign power and then another. It was a spirit of freedom, a desire to rule their own destinies, or at least to be treated as equals in the concert of nations.

The progress of an educated class in these countries, slow but nevertheless growing, produced a new generation of nationalists. They were often misled, used by ruthless politicians for their own ends, but their intentions were clear and could not be ignored. They wanted a voice in their own affairs and resented others dominating them.

In Egypt, Palestine, Syria, Lebanon, and Iraq, the new crop of nationalists was mainly the product of an education introduced into these countries by foreign powers. From them rose new writers and a new class that had to be taken into consideration. From the West they learned about democracy and read about the struggle for freedom in other countries. And they clamored for their own liberty. What they lacked in organisation and level-headed thinking, they made up in volume and enthusiasm. They had their shortcomings. As always, the danger of nationalism is chauvinism. The Arabs fell victim to that, and often these excesses boomeranged.

And here is where Britain committed one of its worst blunders in the Middle East. Rather than be flexible and change with the times, the British in this part of the world persisted in trying to maintain their hold by domination rather than by friendship.

Gradually, two distinct types of Arab political groups developed—the older generation still bowing to Britain's commands, and the new generation standing up to defend their own rights and insisting on speaking their word.

This was one of the reasons why the Arab world had split into two blocs. Because the British were backing those who listened to their word and who cooperated in blind faith with them. This group included King Abdullah of Jordan and the ruling group in Iraq.

Then there was the other group that insisted on being treated as equals and wanted to run matters themselves. By lacking sympathy and understanding for this group, Britain lost many potentially useful friends. In this group were such men as Egypt's King Farouk—then a proud young man refusing to be told what he had to do. His whole background trained him to become a ruler and not a puppet, and had Britain been wise, it would have had him as a friend rather than antagonize him and get involved in many squabbles that could have been easily avoided.

Out of the resentment that grew among many educated Arabs against Britain, the British drew up their policy for those countries. This was to support the aggrandisement of the loyal Hashemites at the expense of the other Arab leaders ruling the various states.

A curious cycle had started in 1916. Then the Arabs were all united in one aim—to get rid of their Turkish overlords and create a united Arab kingdom. The British promised them that if they fought with them against the Turks and Germans, they would be rewarded. They did, but found themselves carved up into many states placed under mandate to Britain and France.

Gradually Arab feeling for onc state faded, and in its place there came a national consciousness of the Syrian for Syria, the Lebanese for Lebanon, and so forth. They felt a kinship with each other, as say, Britain does for the United States. They spoke the same language, but just as the Englishman scoffs at the American's pronunciation, so did the Egyptian at the Iraqi's.

For many years they struggled individually, and their rate of progress differed. Some advanced more rapidly than others towards their goal of political independence. They varied in their standards of living. Each country concentrated on its own problems and tried to achieve the dignity of a sovereign state.

France and England, whose mandate from the League of Nations was to aid these countries on the road to self-government by helping them to reach a sufficiently high standard of development, stood in the way of their freedom. Both powers had developed economic and other advantages in these countries. They could not abide to change their habit of running affairs without question.

The Second World War came, and the two powers paid for their uncompromising attitude towards the Arabs. Rather than have friendly allies, they had unsympathetic neutrals who watched battles fought on their own soil without lifting a hand. They "granted" bases to England and France because they had treaty obligations, but few Arabs watched the world conflict with anything but a feeling of disinterestedness. Some even went as far as allying themselves with the Italians and Germans, saying that perhaps those powers would be better than the others and fulfill their promises of independence to the Arabs. "Anything for a change," they argued.

There were those who believed that despite the shortcomings of British foreign policy, the Arabs should side with the democracies, but they could not find many supporters among the masses. The neutrals or pro-Axis elements had tremendous ammunition to back their arguments. They listed all the "betrayals" and broken promises of the British and French. The supporters of democracy retorted that above all else, democracy was sacred. "Sure, but the British and French are only democratic in their own homes. What have we seen of their principles of democracy here?" asked the others.

As the war receded from the Middle East, a new feeling started sweeping the Arab world—a feeling certainly approved and even inspired to a great degree by Britain. It was the idea of an Arab federation, some sort of a League of Arab states. Why not have a bloc with a coordinated foreign policy and tackling common problems together? The Arab League was born.

The general principles of the Arab League were approved by all. But almost right from the start there was a difference in interpretation of the word "unity." Some wanted to annex the neighboring Arab states, others merely wanted the existing Arab nations to work together.

While the Arab League had its growing pains, the individual Arab governments were still tackling their own national problems with Britain. Egypt wanted British troops to leave the country entirely and particularly to evacuate the cities of Cairo and Alexandria. The British turned a deaf ear to the demands and pleas of the Egyptians. The Iraqis clamoured for the same thing. They got no satisfaction.

In Syria and Lebanon, the British tried to supplant the French. They succeeded in helping the nationals to get rid of the French in the two countries and then tried to infiltrate themselves. But they met a stubborn opposition. Only King Abdullah in Amman and the Hashemites in Baghdad remained loyal friends.

Pressure and compromise due to agitation forced the British to make some concessions to the nationalists in the various countries. But they had won the enmity of many Arab leaders again, and there was a wave of anti-British feeling throughout the Middle East. Only among the Hashemites did the British feel secure.

So once again the Hashemites' dream of a united Arab kingdom came on to the scene. And the cold war between Arabs began. Innumerable intrigues started as a Jihad (Holy War) in Palestine developed into a series of treacheries by one Arab country against the other, and there were coups d'état and attempted coups and several dramatic assassinations. All these were aimed at either bringing about or frustrating a united Arab state.

At that time every Arab leader and most of the political groups opposed communism and readily agreed that unity among the Arabs and an alliance with the west was useful, even vital. But whereas some accepted that unity on any terms the British would propose, there were others who insisted that an alliance with Britain must be based on equality and not subjugation.

The British leaders apparently felt that it would be easier to deal with the blindly loyal Hashemites than the sensitive "independents." Occasionally there seemed to be a change of opinion and then a sudden switch back to the old policy.

Had Britain and the Arabs found a formula to strike it off together, many observers felt that the tension in this part of the world would have disappeared. But the masses became more anti-Britain, and only a few of the rulers remained friendly to them.

Many believed that the United States must step into the Middle East with a sympathetic approach and help the Arabs achieve their freedom. But subsequent American help to the Zionist cause neutralized any real friendship between the United States and the Arab peoples.

IX
Syria—1945

A short, plump man wearing a professorial pince-nez and the uniform of a French general stared at the faces of about thirty expressionless, rather hostile men and women dressed in the uniforms of British and American war correspondents. The man was General Paul Etienne Beynet, "délégué et plenipotentiaire de France au Levant."

The date: June 9, 1945. The place: The beautiful pine-scented residence of the French délégué in Beirut, Lebanon. The reporters there were mostly men and women who had covered the French shelling of Damascus on May 28 and the two subsequent days. Previously, they had watched for one month murders, reprisals, and rioting all over Syria. This month-long rioting had been the prelude to the bombardment of the Syrian capital.

While bombs had dropped, members of allied nations were meeting in San Francisco, planning the peace and talking of the wonderful time the United Nations was going to give to all.

Meanwhile, in Beirut, General Beynet cleared his throat, glanced round seeking the moral support of his staff, and faced the cold looks of the press. For the most part they had been decidedly anti-French, and his job was to convert them. It was not going to be easy. Many of them had been in Damascus and had dodged shot and shell that Frenchmen and their Senegalese janissaries had pumped into their hotel. Again Beynet cleared his throat and addressed the silent group: "Gentlemen: I have asked you to come and see me this morning because it seems to me that faced by so much news of various and sometimes partial sources, it would be useful in the general interest if I gave you a chronological account of the facts which have occurred in Syria from the twelfth to the thirty-first of May.

"Back from Paris on the twelfth of May, I handed over to the Syrian and Lebanese ministers on the eighteenth in Damascus, the aide-mémoire drawn up according to the instructions of my government and which carried the suggestions which were to be the general outline for the opening of the negotiations.

"The way those suggestions were received by Mr. Henri Pharaon (then Lebanese foreign minister) and Djemil Mardam (then Syrian premier and foreign minister) left me with a favorable impression as to the negotiations which were to follow. Those suggestions were, I must say, much more liberal in their conception than any of the treaties linking Great Britain with the other Arab states.

"Therefore I was very astonished when, two days later, both governments informed me of their refusal to go on with the negotiations. This refusal was based, for one thing, on the very terms of our proposals, and for the other, because pressure was supposed to have been used against the two governments.

"This pressure was alluded to the arrival on the cruiser *Jeanne d'Arc* of five hundred not-yet-trained FFI (French Forces of the Interior). I add to be more accurate that on the ninth of May, therefore, before my own return from Paris, a first man of war landed one battalion of Senegalese troops in replacement of another one, a movement which left us with 105 men less than before.

"Gentlemen, I leave it up to your judgement to decide if the arrival of five hundred young men, untrained soldiers, should be regarded as a measure of intimidation.

"From the next day on, a tension started. In Aleppo, individual aggressions began against French military personnel. On

May twentieth, we lost in that city a sublieutenant, murdered at ten A.M. while going to mass, one military policeman, and one Senegalese soldier.

"On the twenty-first of May, the Syrian minister of foreign affairs adopted in the House a vigorous position against the French proposals. The next day, Mr. Henri Pharaon followed his steps in the Lebanese Parliament.

"However, I must emphasize that the French aide-mémoire, which I had so far refrained from making public, out of courtesy towards the Syrian and Lebanese governments, had never been disclosed by them, no doubt on account of their very moderation, of which I make you judge by reading them out to you:

" 'The first step taken by the Fighting French authorities arriving in 1941 in the Levant states was to declare the independence of Syria and Lebanon. This independence has now, in consequence, been acquired. France is glad that her initiative may have borne such happy results. Her hope is that no hindrance and no obstacle of any kind will hamper the full authority of the Syrian and Lebanese governments.

" 'It is in the same spirit, and without any reservation to the independence of Syria and Lebanon, that the French government wishes to secure, so far as it is concerned, the protection of those essential interests which France has kept in Syria and the Lebanon. Those interests are of three types: Cultural, economic, and strategic.

" 'The cultural positions, common to Syria and France, could be defined and guaranteed by a university convention.

" 'The mutual economical positions could be defined and guaranteed by the various agreements usually applied to those matters by traditional international procedure (consular convention, commercial agreements, etc. . . .).

" 'As for the strategical positions they could consist of bases assuring the safeguard of the communications of France and her overseas possessions.

" 'When agreement will have been reached on those three points, the French government will be ready to hand over to the states the troupes spécials (local levies). However, those troops will remain under French high command as long as circumstances do not allow a completely free national command.'

"What I meant by that last sentence, and I so told the ministers of foreign affairs, is that French command could not do without a right of supervision over those local levies as long as France is responsible for security in those states towards the Supreme Allied Command, that is to say, in fact, until the end of the war in the Far East and the dissolution of that Inter-Allied General Staff.

"At the same time, a well-organized and systematical press campaign was backing the point of view of both governments, urging public opinion to take sides and calling on the local levies to desert.

"I want to stress that in order to avoid all incidents, all our troops had been for several days confined to their barracks.

"From May twenty-third on, provocations increased. Isolated positions were attacked, their defenders savagely murdered. In Aleppo, where order had been completely restored, the citadel was evacuated, with the sole purpose of avoiding incidents and in complete agreement with the Syrian authorities. In Damascus, the French command, faced with a growing tension, decided to concentrate its strength in certain points according to plans.

"The following days, individual aggressions and attacks against our communications (supply columns, dispatch riders, telephone lines) increased. To take one instance, one of our columns was attacked on its way from Homs to Hama when carrying supplies to our garrison which had previously withdrawn to their barracks outside the town. The losses on our side were three men killed, one armored car and two lorries destroyed.

"Finally, a general attack was launched on the twenty-ninth of May by the Syrian gendarmerie. I want to point out that the gendarmerie took action against us in Deir el Zor at six-thirty P.M., in Damascus against all our positions at seven-twelve P.M., and in Deraa and Ezraa a few minutes before eight P.M.

"Here again, gentlemen, I leave it up to you to decide whether such perfect timing in action could be the result of mere coincidence.

"In Deraa and Ezraa, our positions were overcome. In the Djebel Druze, in spite of all our officers being arrested at dawn, neither the population nor the troopers could be induced to one single hostile deed towards the French. At the same time, all our positions were firmly held in Damascus.

"One single plane flies over the citadel, headquarters of the gendarmerie and center of the attack, and drops three bombs of 250 pounds each. One battery, that is to say, four field guns, opens fire against the gathering points of the attacking forces.

"On the thirtieth, Deir el Zor is looted by a tribe after French forces have been evacuated to barracks south of the town. Two French military policemen and a French woman are killed, her naked body being dragged through the streets and finally thrown in the Euphrates.

"The French troops in Damascus, faced with the alternative of either being slaughtered or to occupy the positions of the gendarmerie, take over the Parliament House, turned into an ammunition depot by the gendarmerie, the town hall, the Bank of Syria, the Serail (government building), the general post office, and clear the Avenue de la Victoire up to the Souk Hamadie. Our troops are supported by the same plane dropping three bombs of twenty-five pounds and by artillery fire.

"As such measures had to be carried out in a densely populated town, death of innocent beings could not be avoided. I insist on expressing how painful it has been to the French representatives to find themselves compelled to undertake an action which has brought so much sorrow. But I wish to stress also, as I said before, that such action was undertaken by only one plane and one battery, that is to say, that we deliberately restricted this action to its minimum.

"On that Wednesday night at eleven P.M. in Paris, General de Gaulle ordered the cease-fire. In fact, the next day, operations came to an end everywhere. An air action brought Deir el Zor back to calm around two P.M., and at six P.M. the mohafez (governor) and the colonel commanding the gendarmerie offered their submission.

"The same thing happened in Damascus which the government had left, when the chiefs of districts entered into negotiations with the commander of the French garrison.

"The Djebel squadrons were regrouping spontaneously under French command. On that same day at eight P.M., the British ultimatum disclosed in London at twelve and received in Paris at one-thirty P.M., was handed over to the general commandant superieur by General Pilleau.

"In fact, gentlemen, as you may see, fire had ceased several hours before the British intervention, and we had the situation in hand.

"I would like to stress that before the British government's intervention was known, the British commander in chief in the Middle East (Sir Bernard Paget), had thought fit to cut off the rations supplied by the British military authorities to the French troops, according to an agreement in force since several years.

"I wanted to relate in your presence the chronological succession of events up to the moment when, following instructions of his government, General Paget was considered responsible for the maintenance of order.

"May I add that the following days, the rioters and the gendarmerie thought themselves encouraged to start again hostile acts which have cost us up to now over a dozen killed. This is all the more explainable that for a few days we were expressly refused the right of self-defence in case of aggression and that the British guns were aimed at our barracks.

"As for the deeper and wider causes of the crisis, may I ask you gentlemen to read over the statement of the head of the French government, which will be handed over to you with the text of my own declaration."

This was the story that the correspondents heard in silence. It was neither the full story nor was it a completely accurate one. Many of them had lived through these days and did not agree with the statements by General Beynet. A shower of hands went up and questions were fired at the poor man defending the French shelling of Damascus on May 28, which heralded the end of France in Syria and a new low in Anglo-French relations.

The questions came fast and furious: "Were the French troops merely undertaking legitimate self-defence, and does the general not believe that the French answer, consisting of the shelling of the city, was a disproportionate measure to the cause of the trouble?" asked one correspondent who had been through the shelling.

Beynet answered: "I have asked for an inquiry. . . ."

"Why was the Orient Palace subject to shelling and machine-gun fire?" indignantly asked another correspondent who had been living there.

"Perhaps it was because rifle shots came from the Orient Palace," suggested Beynet.

"Were there any Syrian gendarmes in the hotel?"

"I was not there, but I believe that all the buildings of that square were occupied by the gendarmes. You gentlemen can go to Damascus and get your information from disinterested, objective persons. But make a conscientious inquiry." The poor man did not seem to know that at least one-third of the correspondents there had witnessed the whole thing, knew that no shots had been fired from the Orient Palace where they were living, and that there had been no gendarmes there.

Many more questions snapped out. Had British agents been behind this Syrian affair? It was not in Beynet's competence to answer this, but a question for the French provisional government. By implication, we understood that there had been British agents at work.

"Was it really the only way to settle this conflict, once it had started, by shelling and bombing?"

"We had to react or let ourselves by massacred," he answered. "When the Allies in 1944 bombed the towns of France—which no Frenchman reproached them for doing—do you think they could do otherwise?" No one could understand the comparison.

"Do you think that the uprisings in Syria are spontaneous reactions against the French, or do you believe that they are provoked by others?"

"I think that the two factors can be included. Such events are not simple. In all towns in the world a part of the population can be moved to riot. And also, where there are conflicting interests, it is not surprising that the result is deplorable."

There were many more, and of various types. The story of the shelling of Damascus was the outcome of a fresh crop of troubles. This was not the first time the French had shelled the city. Ever since France obtained a mandate over Syria, the nationalists in Damascus who had hoped for a united Arab kingdom with Damascus as the capital had bitterly fought France, sometimes by passive resistance, and at others, violently. There had been several uprisings, riots, and long wars. Most famous, the Druze campaigns of 1925–1926.

But this most recent crisis started, as General Beynet stated, on May 12, 1945, when the French delegate returned to Beirut from Paris carrying what the French thought were liberal terms to offer the Levant states for the signing of a treaty that would give France cultural, economical, and strategical privileges in Syria and Lebanon. The two countries had been promised their independence in 1941. Lebanon had fought for it in 1943 and obtained a measure of satisfaction. Now the time had come to settle the matter finally. France thought her terms for treaties were attractive. They were perhaps better than Britain had offered most of her Arab allies. But France forgot that she was a much weakened nation and that Britain was at the moment cooperating with the Arabs to the detriment of the French position in the Levant.

On May 18, Beynet handed his terms to the Syrians and Lebanese. On the twenty-first, Syrian foreign minister Djemil Mardam rejected them, and throughout Syria the trouble that had started from the eighteenth, increased.

General strikes, accompanied by rioting and loss of lives, spread in Syria and Lebanon, and a tension grew throughout the Arab world.

Several persons were killed in the Levant, and French Senegalese troops were reported to have fired on demonstrators who were burning French cooperative stores. British stores nearby were not molested.

Some seventeen persons were wounded in clashes in Damascus, where the worst situation had developed. In the Syrian towns of Homs, Hama, and Aleppo, clashes were reported between French and Syrians. From Jerusalem came news that the Arabs had called a one-day strike in support of Lebanon and Syria.

Both Lebanon and Syria appealed to the United States and Great Britain for support and to the new and then potentially powerful Arab League. Immediately the league offered them its backing.

Abdel Rahman Azzam Bey (later Pasha) said in a statement in Cairo that the League might hold a special meeting on behalf of Syria and Lebanon. He charged the French had reinforced their troops in the country merely to back her position and that her latest proposals were "reactionary, outdated, and represented an imperialistic, colonial frame of mind." He said: "Arab states, backed by public opinion and the whole Muslim world, will stand for liberty and the right of self-determination. The Arab League will not fail in its duty to stand firm and safeguard the liberty and independence of any threatened league member.''

United states minister George Wadsworth conferred with local leaders in Beirut. The stage was set for another serious crisis in the Arab world which would considerably change the state of affairs in this area and have repercussions for many a year.

X
The Crisis

I had hardly landed in Beirut than I was made aware that a worse crisis than 1943 was on. It was serious, and friends told me that it was even worse in Damascus. Already there was a good deal of fighting in various towns of Syria, and the Lebanese were starting to organize their youth movements and political parties into fighting units.

France, through Gen. Paul Etienne Beynet, had delivered an aide-mémoire listing the various privileges she sought in the Levant. At that particular moment when Beynet was negotiating with the foreign ministers of Syria and Lebanon, a French warship unloaded some 500 French soldiers at Beirut. Another warship soon followed, landing Senegalese. Whether this was merely routine troop movements, as the French later stated, or a threatening move to intimidate the local governments, the appearance of new French soldiers only served to infuriate the local inhabitants. This was perhaps one of the unwisest French moves at the time.

Had the French authorities studied the Syrian and Lebanese mentality of the moment, they would have quickly realized they were committing a grave error. The two small nations were in no mood to be bullied. They felt they were backed by the British and possibly the Americans. The Russians were courting them. They felt proud that they were being represented at the United Nations meeting in San Francisco, and for the first time in many years, were being placed on an equal footing with the other nations of the world.

If the French were genuine in their subsequent explanation that this was merely a routine affair of exchange of troops, they were guilty of a grave diplomatic blunder. They should have known better than to send troops at a delicate time when they were negotiating a treaty. Surely they could have guessed that the hypersensitive Syrians and Lebanese would interpret this as an effort to intimidate them. And even had they failed to recognize this, there were agents provocateurs who would have incited the masses to protest. Whatever it was, this arrival of French warships and troops was the straw which broke the camel's back. What little discontent, what minor rioting there was quickly swelled into a series of murders, clashes, strikes, and retaliation.

The first reports to reach me on my arrival in Beirut were that the situation was very tense and more trouble was expected. A British officer who had just returned to Beirut from Damascus said, "I have been in five revolutions, but never have I seen a situation as tense as in Syria."

French sources told me that they were doing their utmost to avoid any trouble or incidents, and had withdrawn all their troops to their barracks, and had concentrated most French families into one area in readiness to evacuate them should the situation worsen. The troubles were already getting out of hand in Homs and Hama, although it was still relatively quiet in Damascus and Aleppo. Some elements were in favor of holding their horses until the outcome of meetings then taking place in Paris between General de Gaulle and the British and American ambassadors. Others stated that they should allow the newly formed Arab League to handle the matter, and still others wondered whether it might not be the first test case for the United Nations meeting at San Francisco.

In Damascus itself, the Syrian Parliament met to see what it should do about the rapidly growing crisis. Certainly there was trouble everywhere. Syrian raiders had attacked the French garrisons at Deraa and Ezraa, and after a bitter fight had captured the forts. In Damascus, tension was rising. Stories of incidents started pouring in. A group of students had poured a barrel of oil on a French officer and set him alight. There were other stories of French troops shooting up demonstrators.

French soldiers were gathered in their barracks, and a strong force was stationed in and around the house of General Oliva-Roget, the French commander. This house was just opposite the Syrian Parliament. On May 29, 1945, at about 6:30 in the evening, there was a roar of artillery fire as the French army opened its attack.

From that moment on, nobody could get a full, accurate picture of what happened in this historic capital. It just depended on where you happened to be. The French forces quickly brought seventy-five millimetre cannons up to the gates of the Syrian Parliament and blasted away. The local gendarmes on duty were rapidly overpowered. In other parts of the city, spurts of dust and explosions showed that the French were hammering away.

Most of the battle went on in the heart of Damascus. The fashionable suburbs, inhabited by many of the foreign communities, were not damaged. But curiously, the Orient Palace Hotel, situated near the railway station and in a square not far from one of the French barracks, received the closest attention of the French artillery and machine gunners. Most of the residents of this hotel happened to be British officers, a few Russian diplomats, and Anglo-American war correspondents. They were all forced to lie flat on their faces as mortars, seventy-five-millimetre shells, and heavy machine-gun bullets ripped through the main lobbies and through the bedroom windows.

A British army major and another British officer were hit. The major died. Just outside the hotel, the French set up a battery of mortars and seventy-fives to pound the densely populated old quarter of the Souk Hamidieh, favourite haunt of European tourists searching for the famed Damascus brocade and old silver.

From his sick bed, Pres. Shukry el Kuwatly, suffering from severe stomach ulcers, sent an urgent appeal to the British and American ministers in Beirut to intervene. The Syrians were unable to put up much of a defence. Their machine guns and rifles were inadequate against planes, cannons, and the well-organized efficiency of the French.

The French sources I contacted told me that the Syrians had started the attack and that they then replied firmly. "We were instructed never to attack the population unless we were provoked, but once provoked we should strike hard, crush any opposition, and restore order." They certainly struck hard and committed another grave blunder in French Middle Eastern diplomacy.

Syrian officials assured me that the French had started shelling and that their retaliation was out of all proportion to the incidents caused by Syrian nationalists. I certainly agreed about the retaliation being out of all proportion. The Syrian government also assured me that they had been telling their people not to start any trouble and give the Arab League a chance to settle this problem amicably. But there was no stopping some of the extremist elements.

Within a few minutes of the beginning of the bombardment, the Syrian Parliament was gutted, the Bank of Syria seriously damaged, and the cable office destroyed. Many of the correspondents in Damascus were pinned down in their quarters by shell fire. Even diplomats could hardly move, if they happened to be in the centre of the town. United States consul William Porter was able to move around in an armored car. (In an absentminded moment, he put his hand on the red-hot exhaust of his vehicle, and severely burned his arm.) Porter often went to see the ailing President Kuwatly and various members of the Syrian government.

On the second day of the shelling of Damascus, the British military authorities arranged a truce between Syrians and French, in order to evacuate all British and American families from the capital. From 4:00 P.M. to 6:00 P.M., the city was strangely quiet as both sides looked on while cars containing frightened Anglo-American children streamed out of town. Then the fight was on again. It attracted worldwide attention and saw British-manned, American-made tanks swivelling their guns on Frenchmen before it subsided.

XI
The Rape of Damascus

The storied city was strangely quiet during the truce arranged to evacuate British and American children from Damascus. During that period of quiet, I managed to slip into Damascus again and head for the comparative security of the suburb where the British army garrison was billeted. There, too, was the house of British minister Terrence Shone and the president of the Republic.

With Maj. Richard Wyndham, later to be killed in Palestine and then acting as special correspondent for a British weekly, we headed for the residence of Colonel Stirling. He was an old friend of Wyndham's and would give us the latest picture of the fighting and political developments. When we got to the house, Colonel Stirling was not there. He was in conference at Mr. Shone's.

We waited for a while, then walked up the hill towards the British legation, just a few hundred yards away. The top officials were in conference and the other legation officials were rushing around with messages and files. Dispatch riders were coming in and out, the secretaries dashed through the legation on jobs for their superiors. Outside, two menacing-looking British armored cars stood on guard.

While we waited, Dick Wyndham told me something about Colonel Stirling. This was the same Stirling who had been a companion of the legendary Lawrence of Arabia in the First World War. He had taken part in the Arab struggle for independence, knew most of the Arab leaders from their younger fighting days, and was on intimate terms with them now that they were the rulers of the country.

Between one world war and another, Stirling had had his ups and downs. Reports had reached his old friends that he had become so poor, he worked as a hotel porter in London, and then went to work for an oil company in Rumania. He had got to know the Central European states almost as well as he knew the deserts and tribes of the Middle East.

The Second World War saw him appointed assistant military attaché in Turkey. It was from there that Stirling used to slip into German-occupied Europe and carry out missions that would have frightened many a younger man. His years with the oil company in Rumania stood him in good stead, and he was able to contribute substantially to the work of sabotaging enemy installations and getting valuable information.

Stories were told of his exploits there. One incident was the time when Stirling went into Rumania carrying limpet mines to stick on Nazi vessels in Black Sea ports. When he entered the coach on one of the Rumanian trains, a youthful German officer took pity on the small middle-aged man struggling with a heavy package and helped him with his bag. There were other tales on how he, with others, engineered the escape from Rumania of various personalities who could be useful to the Allies.

When the European war was over, Colonel Stirling was transferred to Damascus where he occupied the post of director of frontiers and tribes with the British army. This gave him a chance to renew his old acquaintance with the desert and the people of the area.

Stirling came out of the meeting to greet his friend Wyndham and spent a few minutes giving us a brief picture of the situation. He confirmed what we already knew—that it was dangerous to try to get to the Orient Palace for accommodation and that, anyway, it was under fire and the cable office destroyed. So it was useless for correspondents. He suggested we stay at his house, which was empty, as he was staying with the British minister. He authorized us to use his telephone, which was connected to a British military line, and therefore, free of the Franco-Syrian censorship and, as far as he knew, still operating.

We jumped at his offer and made our way to his house. The sun was setting as we walked quickly away. The truce was just about over. While we were in the streets, the first guns started barking again, and the fight went on.

In reality, it was too one-sided to be called a fight. Many have called it the Rape of Damascus, and that was what it had become. French shells screamed through the air and landed in the thickly populated native quarters of the city. Machine guns opened up with quick, murderous bursts, and occasionally from the Syrians came a few answering shots.

Stirling's house gave us a ringside view of the fighting. In the rapidly failing light we could follow the course of the shelling. The French guns were on the outskirts of the city to our right and the shells whined past us to explode below and to the left of us.

As we sat, an old man in Bedouin clothes slowly entered the courtyard of the house and asked for Stirling. We told him he was not there, so he sat down.

He gave us some news of the town. "The French are shelling houses at point-blank range and machine-gunning occupants as they rush out. It is very bad." This old man was very laconic about it all and did not seem either very disturbed by the shelling or excited by its implications. Neither did he seem in any way frightened by the shells which shook the house. He just sat there, smoking a cigarette.

"This is not the first time this city has been thus bombed by the French, and I have seen too much fighting to be affected by it," he said, in answer to my question as to how he could stay so calm.

"My fighting days are over," he said, "but in my time I have fought with Lawrence." There was quiet pride and affection when he said this. "Yes, I have known Stirling from those days. Lawrence and I were good friends." We were interrupted by several explosions, louder and closer than usual. I wondered whether the French might not be hitting this suburb despite the presence of British troops and houses of various diplomatic missions. After all, they had smashed the Orient Palace, and they might be tempted to wipe out Stirling's house. They hated Stirling. They knew he felt that the Syrians should have their independence and had already accused him of being behind the rioting Syrian nationalists.

Suddenly the old Bedouin spoke again: "Lawrence even took me to England with him on one occasion. He took me to the house of a great lady who was a friend of his, or perhaps a relative. She was supposed to be a very beautiful lady. And Lawrence asked me whether I thought her beautiful too. Because he was my friend, I answered frankly that I thought the maid who was serving us tea was much more attractive and desirable. She had more flesh to her than the supposedly beautiful lady."

This reminiscing took our minds off the continuous bombardment that shook the city. He enjoyed talking more than I enjoyed listening to him. He might have been a seasoned warrior, but I felt myself wishing that I did not have to translate his stories to Wyndham. I wanted to think about the shelling near us.

The French were now using star shells to light up the city so that they could see the effects of their bombing. Wyndham said: "Let's go up to the roof to get a better view of the shelling."

Reluctantly I got up and followed him. The old man got up too, and said, "If you are going up to the roof, you'd better be careful. Both the French and the Syrian snipers might shoot at you." With this encouraging remark, we clambered up the stairs to the roof. It was dark when we got there. In the distance was the red glow of fires burning in the city. A few minutes later, the darkness disappeared as another star shell burst and clearly lit the area. We got a quick view of smoking buildings and shadows flitting through the street. Then more explosions, machine gun bursts, and the crack of rifles. There was a sudden rush of air between Wyndham and me, like a startled bat hurtling between us. "What was that?" I asked, as if I didn't know.

"Let's get out of here. They're shooting at us," answered Dick. The old sheikh followed us down, taking his time to show his contempt of the snipers. "They're bad shots. they should have got at least one of us when they transformed the night into day," he said.

When we got back to the relative security of the courtyard, I started worrying about sending a story to my office. It had been some hours since my return to Damascus, and I was worried that other correspondents might have sent messages while I sat just watching shells bursting and houses crumbling. Stirling had told us that there were several war correspondents pinned down in the Orient Palace, and Dick and I were wondering whether they had been able to send off any cables during the last few hectic hours.

I jotted down all the notes I could think of and made my way to the room where Stirling kept his telephone. It was situated by a window overlooking the no-man's-land area. Blithely I turned on the light as I walked into the room and headed for the telephone. It was a military line connecting the British garrison in Damascus to other garrisons in the Middle East. Civilian lines were tapped by the French. I sat at my vantage point and twirled the handle of the ancient apparatus. Almost immediately an alert, respectful voice came on the line. "Yes, sir?"

In my best military tone I barked out the number of the United Press office in Jerusalem and told him to put me through. At that moment Wyndham came barging in and turned off the light.

"You silly fool, do you want to get shot? You're making a perfect target framed in that bloody window with all that light behind you."

Just then Jerusalem came through, and I didn't have any more time to argue. All the carefully written notes were junked, and I dictated my story from memory. The events of the afternoon, the fill-in by Stirling, the reports on the shooting-up of the Orient Palace, and my eyewitness account of the shelling still proceeding before us.

On the other end somebody in the Jerusalem office took down my dictation efficiently, injecting an exclamation every now and then as he heard over the telephone the explosions and machine guns rattling. I told him to rush that story through censorship and on to London as quickly as possible and started giving him more details, as I remembered them, when the line went dead.

There was still so much more I wanted to dictate, so many things I suddenly remembered that I angrily shook the phone.

The English operator at the barracks nearby came on again. "Sorry, sir, either the wogs or the frogs have cut the bloody line, begging your pardon, sir."

There was nothing else to do, and I just had to wait until next morning. We decided to turn in and try and get some sleep, as both of us anticipated a considerable amount of activity next day. But sleep was not an easy thing as shells kept bursting and bullets flying through the night. We did get some sleep, in spite of it all, and were awake at the crack of dawn next day.

We went over to British headquarters where we saw the reports sent in by various British military observers. Signal corps had maintained radio communication with these observers and with headquarters in Cairo, and we pleaded in vain to be allowed to send some messages immediately over their radio to Cairo. The commanding officer explained that they had too many military and official messages to send to allow us transmit any new stories but promised us to send something later during the day.

There was much to do and see during that day. We called on the British minister and Colonel Stirling to get news of any developments and were told of various reports that had reached them. Britain and the United States were very concerned with the developments in Damascus, and the Arab League had summoned a hasty meeting in Cairo. There were strikes of sympathy in Beirut and among the Palestine Arabs. In Homs and Hama and other towns in Syria, there had been clashes between French troops and the Syrians. French planes had bombed Hama, said one report, and one plane had been shot down by rifle fire from the Syrians.

In London, Foreign Secretary Anthony Eden had told the House of Commons that Britain had taken the initiative in trying to improve the situation in Syria where the arrival of French reinforcements had shaken the whole Arab world. Eden said he wanted to see what results were achieved before reporting on steps taken by the British.

Stirling also suggested that we go up the road to visit Wing Commander Dudley Marsack, who was information officer. We went to Marsack's, another of those colorful British figures who played such vital roles without appearing to have anything to do with the whole matter.

Dudley Marsack, a New Zealander in the British Royal Air Force, had long since adopted the Muslim faith and named himself Nour el Din Marsack. He spoke excellent Arabic and was on intimate terms with all the Syrian nationalists and political leaders. He had a brother who had also become a Muslim and was "somewhere" in the Middle East.

I found Marsack to be a short, rosy-cheeked man with alert eyes that belied the cherubic innocence of his face. His Syrian assistants evidently worshipped him, and he was certainly a hustler. He promised to arrange some meetings for us with various Syrian leaders later that day.

We went back to British headquarters to see whether we could send any messages to our offices, but still the transmitters were busy. As we walked there we saw a French plane heading towards the city. It roared over us and then swooped low as it dived towards the native part of Damascus. Then we saw a stick of bombs hurtling down and explode. Lazily the plane circled and came in for another run. The Syrians had no defence against planes and the aircraft was able to approach without any danger of being fired upon by anything bigger than a light machine gun or a rifle. Again bombs dropped, and the plane circled overhead waiting for the smoke and dust to clear to see and possibly photograph the damage done.

I thought of the meeting place then at San Francisco where the United Nations was gathering for the first time to lay the foundations of peace and friendship among the anti-Axis forces. Even now, I thought, French delegates were calmly sitting discussing principles of peace and humanity while their soldiers were smashing this beautiful, historic city, supposed to be the oldest in the world.

An unnamed British officer told us he had urged the French commander, General Oliva Roget, to stop the "inhuman carnage." By that time, there were two big fires and several smaller ones burning fiercely in the city.

Suddenly the firing died down and only an occasional rifle shot or burst of machine-gun fire jarred the deadly quiet. We decided to ask the British commander for a lift in one of his armored cars to tour the devastated city and see for ourselves the damage. Surprisingly, the commander accepted. We piled into the armored car and roared away.

From the relative security of our suburban shelter, we slowly rolled into the "target area." Here and there we saw the ruins of a house destroyed by shells or gutted by fire. There was no life in the streets. As we approached the Orient Palace hotel we saw that it had been badly hit. We stood in the turret, taking stock of the situation. Not far from the hotel, near the railway station of the Damascus-Djeddah line, were the French barracks.

We saw that a mortar and a machine gun were placed in the avenue just outside the barracks. Both were pointed in the direction of the "souk" at the end of the road. Senegalese troops manned the gun, while a French officer, cigarette dangling from the corner of his mouth, leaned against a tree.

As we approached him he dropped his hand, and the two guns went into action, as though for our benefit. From where we were we could not see exactly what they were shooting at, but we could only see smoking houses in the distance and presumed they were training their guns on these buildings at the far end of the street. We were right in our assumption. The French officer, still leaning against the tree, explained that he had instructions to keep the Syrians pinned in their area, and destroy any centres of resistance. He advised us not to go any further as we might run into trouble.

We said we would risk it and go on, but he insisted that he could not allow us through unless we had a permit.

"We don't have a permit."

"Then go and get one, but you don't pass without it," he retorted.

We did not want to complicate matters, and, anyway, there was more to see in other directions, so we made off into another part of the city. It was the same story everywhere we went. Damaged or destroyed houses, no life, shutters flapping in the wind, doors swinging open and shut.

On our return to our area we again met Marsack who had some news for us. He had arranged a meeting with Jamil Mardam, acting prime minister. The premier then was Saadallah el Jabry, who was in Cairo attending the Arab League meeting on Syria. At the same time one of Marsack's assistants informed us that there were meetings going on in London about the Syrian matter, and that the House of Commons was discussing the Syrian crisis.

Wyndham and I set off to see Mardam bey, and we found a very worried man, with greying hair, seated among many friends and colleagues, getting reports of the damage done to the city. With the absent-minded air of a man who had things of much graver importance to handle Mardam answered some of our questions. He seemed to be very ill at ease, almost shell-shocked. He said that dead and wounded in the last couple of days' bombing must amount to between three thousand and four thousand, and reports were still coming in.

But there were developments in the various world capitals, and the crisis was on the point of being solved. On May 31, with a suddenness that startled the world, the British ordered the French to cease fire, return their troops to their quarters, and announced that British troops were being sent into Syria to handle the matter and restore conditions to normal.

From London we received a report stating, "Great Britain ordered her troops into Syria to halt the bloody Arab-French disorders and served a virtual ultimatum on France to cease hostilities in the Levant immediately.

"In a move to resolve the Levant crisis and prevent a possible rupture of allied communications lines to the Far East, Prime Minister Winston Churchill announced he had ordered British armed intervention between the warring French and Arab forces in Syria and Lebanon."

At the same time a terse memorandum was dispatched to General de Gaulle "requesting" the immediate withdrawal of all French troops in the Levant to their barracks "to avoid collision between British and French forces.

"Once firing has ceased and order has been restored, we shall be prepared to begin tri-partite discussions here in London," the British note said.

The sudden British intervention climaxed three weeks of spreading disorder in the Levant, touched off by the dispatch of French reinforcements to Syria and Lebanon to back up France's demand for strategic bases in the former mandated countries, said the British briefing to correspondents in London.

In the House of Commons, Foreign Secretary Anthony Eden announced that the ancient city of Damascus was aflame from French bombing and shelling and that the situation had gotten worse in the past twelve hours. Eden said that late advices from the British minister in Damascus reported heavy and continued fighting in the city throughout the previous night and early that day.

The British foreign secretary said that British and American civilian colonies were evacuated from Damascus during a brief armistice early in the afternoon of May 30. Continuing his outline of what had happened to oblige the British to order the French cease-fire, Eden said that after the armistice, the centre of the city was subjected to a very heavy and concentrated French artillery bombardment, and French war planes roared in to bomb the Syrian garrison.

Cries of "shame" arose from the House when Eden revealed that bombs had been dropped on the biblical city.

Eden emphasized that Britain had been "immensely anxious" to avoid intervention in the Levant, but he reiterated that the threat to British and American supply lines to the Far Eastern theatre had become too serious a problem to ignore. The British Cabinet, he said, was in constant touch with the United States government on the situation.

Reports from Washington said that Acting Secretary of State Joseph C. Grew told the press that President Truman had approved Great Britain's intervention to end bloodshed in the Levant.

Grew said that the United States government had told France three days before that French representatives appeared to "have been using the threat of force" to obtain special concessions from their former mandates, Syria and Lebanon.

Grew made the note public. It told Gen. Charles de Gaulle's government, "in a most friendly spirit," that it should "review its policy towards Syria and Lebanon with the purpose of finding a way" to show the whole world that France "intends to treat them as fully sovereign and independent members of the family of nations."

The acting secretary of state told a news conference that the United States would consider the use of American lend-lease equipment by French forces in Syria as a violation of the American-French lend-lease agreement. Although Grew did not definitely know whether the French were using lend-lease equipment against the Syrians, observers and correspondents there were quite sure that the Baltimore planes and the guns that were shelling the city were part of the lend-lease agreement.

While these developments were taking place in the world's capitals, Damascus was starting to get the news over the radios. For a while, the firing died down, but suddenly once more machine-gun and rifle fire cracked out again through the city, as French-African troops began looting food shops which had opened for the half-starved native population.

It gradually transpired that following the cease-fire order, the French officers retired to their quarters, leaving Senegalese and Cherkess colonial troops to act as they pleased. The move resulted in the looting of the old souks and marketplaces.

I went through the city again, driving a small truck lent to me by the British army. Wyndham and I drove slowly past the Parliament house where groups of Cherkess were standing idly, their trucks filled with goods they had looted from various shops. Nearing a crossroads, we were caught in a duel between some Senegalese at one side of the street and, on the edge of the souk, Syrians barricaded behind sandbags defending the shops from the would-be looters.

As shots started from both sides, we decided to make a dash for the Syrians behind the sandbags. For a while I shouted at them in Arabic that we were friends and that we wanted to join them. Upon receiving a word of encouragement, we ran across the few metres of exposed terrain and dived over the sandbags to the relative security of the Syrian defences.

We stayed there long enough to get a few photographs of the defenders, and then moved backward through the covered souks into the maze that was Old Damascus. Within a few seconds, there was a crowd of Syrians around us, wanting to know who we were. When they discovered we were correspondents, they all started telling us stories of their nightmarish existence for the last two or three days.

Among the crowd was a young lawyer I had known previously, who volunteered to escort us to the citadel that had been hit by French planes.

As we went through the narrow streets, we could see gaping holes caused by the shelling and got a stream of accounts by people crowding us. They wanted to know whether it was true that the French had been ordered to cease fire. Yes, we answered. But how was it that they were still firing? Because the colonial troops have not obeyed the orders. Would the British and Americans come in to protect the Syrians against the furious French? We did not know.

The Syrians were afraid to come out of their hiding places and return to their homes. Anyway, the town was still teeming with the colonials who wanted to kill and rob on sight, cease-fire or no cease-fire.

By that time, we reached the citadel, which served as barracks, prison, and historical monument. The place was stinking with the sickly stench of death. It choked you by its penetrating odor, and this nauseating, sickening stench stayed with me for many days.

Bodies of Syrian convicts who had been jailed in the citadel lay around the place, already terribly swollen and covered with thousands of flies that buzzed in and out of their wounds. Most of the damage was the result of a direct hit from the French plane that had circled the city. We took a few photographs and went out on the roof to get a view of the city. There was no point in remaining in this horrible, smelly place any longer. So, we went out, escorted by dozens of Damascenes.

From there, I returned to the centre of the town and tried to see General Oliva-Roget, the French commander in Syria. He was the man who was held responsible for the drastic French action in Damascus. It had not been easy to get to him before. He was still in no mood to meet newspapermen, but did not have enough spirit left in him to ward us off. When I saw him, he was a broken, bitter man. He said that British intervention came just at the time when his troops had "tamed" the Syrians and were getting the situation under control. "A few more hours, and there would not have been any problem," he said angrily. His feelings against the British were frank and outspoken. "When the Syrians were assassinating our men, the British did not raise a hand, but now when we had almost completed their submission, they intervene," he said.

Oliva-Roget alleged that the French had never fired on civilians, but I had seen them firing on civilians. In all justice to the man, it was quite likely he did not know what his subalterns were doing, and it is quite likely that they ignored their chief's orders and fired at everything. He said that his troops only fired on known nationalist strongholds, but I pointed out to him that four British casualties had been reported and that the wife of a British church official had been killed by a sniper.

His answer was that Syrian nationalists had probably fired the shots that killed these civilians. "After all," he said, "the British had been giving arms and ammunition to their Syrian friends."

Oliva-Roget's headquarters were just opposite the Parliament buildings that he had ordered smashed in the first moment of the bombing of Damascus. I asked the Frenchman if I could photograph the Parliament and whether he would step outside so that I could photograph him with the destroyed Parliament as a background.

Referring to the Parliament buildings, he said, "I suppose you want the world to see what brutal acts we have committed." I made no answer, but took my photographs and then asked him to pose. He looked at me and said: "And I suppose you will write under this picture, 'And here is the savage who committed this outrage.' "

Nevertheless, he posed, and afterwards turned about on his heel and went indoors with hardly a glance at us.

The people were still frightened and did not dare come out into the streets, although the news that British forces were on their way to take over from the French had spread through the souks like wildfire. Here and there, Syrians started to emerge, and everywhere we went in our correspondents' uniforms, Wyndham and I were cheered and surrounded by crowds of delirious Syrians.

About that time, the British propaganda machine, which had swung into action, sent a military observer to survey the scene and send in a report. A rather excitable captain appeared and told us that his dual job was to conduct the correspondents around, now that Damascus was temporarily placed under British military control, and to write his own reports for public relations. We had been doing quite well without any conducting officer, but we shrugged our shoulders and trailed behind Captain E. Letts. He had a truck, and Wyndham and I felt it would be very useful to be along with him rather than to walk through the streets.

In somewhat flowery terms, Captain Letts produced his first report on June 2. Here it is:

> Peace has been restored to Damascus.
>
> That is the tremendous fact which overrides all others. After almost a week of bloody fighting in which French local troops

apparently went beserk, and with or without knowledge of their superiors, used every type of modern weapons, including planes, tanks, artillery and machine guns against the local unarmed civilian population, the great Syrian capital is now quickly getting back to normal. But it will be many years before the atrocious acts of utter Prussian barbarianism are forgotten by the people.

In the last few years, we have been aware of the ''Montgomery and the Alexander touch''. Now we have the ''Paget touch,'' and it is with cool admiration that we find the C. in C., Middle East, ordered by Mr. Churchill to intervene, flying straight to the scene of the trouble, touring the streets of Damascus, which only a few hours before were cleared of anything except terrified animals and being swept with machine-gun bullets, and receiving tumultuous cheers of the jubilant population. It was the familiar scene of the liberation of Tripoli, Tunis, Rome, Paris and Brussels all over again.

The sound of the incessant clapping of hands, the smiles on the formerly terrified people are still with me. The C. in C. was cheered, but so was every single British soldier who went anywhere in the city immediately it became known that British troops had come in.

The story might have been very different had not wisdom and clear thinking, coupled with stern words, been used by the British. It might have been different too, had not the attitude of the French local troops changed in a few hours from arrogance—and I regret to say, brutality—to one of utter submission, almost cowardice.

I have never seen such a contrast as that presented by Damascus on Friday, June 1st. In the early morning, after a night of desultory firing, I drove a party of war correspondents on a short tour of the centre of the city. Our truck, covered by a large Union Jack, and like all British Army vehicles [that had] appeared in the last few days, it had plates painted with the Union Jack on the front and back.

Nevertheless, this display did not prevent my being threatened with shooting by a French sentry. I looked almost closer down the barrel than I have looked at rifle inspections. Apparently, he thought it wiser not to shoot, and with the correspondents sitting beside me, we passed the bullet-scarred Bank of Syria, Officers' Club, the NAAFI, and Orient Palace (where a British officer had been killed, and another wounded two days previously), and by some burnt out shops and buildings to the damaged souks and the street called Straight.

As we moved slowly along the deserted streets, shots were being fired, as a sniper's battle was being fought. A cat raced across the road in front of us, terrified by the noise. Men stopped behind hastily erected street barricades, loaded rifles in their hands. By the Omayad Mosque, a crowd of Syrians, including many boys, stood behind a barricade, and as the correspondents dismounted, and they saw that one, Major Dick Wyndham was British and the other, Mr. Sam Souki, was American,* they raised a spontaneous cheer.

The other part of the strange contrast of this memorable first of June was in the afternoon, when units of the 3rd King's Own Hussars and the 14th Scinde Horse, followed some hours later by the Foresters, entered the city. As soon as the local people heard the rumble of tanks, and saw the British fully armed and prepared, if need be to fight, they turned out en masse and gave them the same kind of welcome that the crowds of other liberated capitals have given their liberators.

But to appreciate why there were these scenes of joy, the story must be told of the few days that preceded June 1st. It is an ugly story, and one cannot imagine that France—de Gaulle's France—whom the free people of the world love and admire, directed or condoned the acts of savagery which were ruthlessly carried out, not only in Damascus, but in other parts of Syria. They were diabolical, and one could not help but feel that the commander of the French Forces in Syria knew what was going on, and had ordered the direct attacks of the civilian population without some fore thought and planning.

---

* Although not an American, I was accredited to the U.S. forces and wore an American uniform. Hence Lett's error.

Probably this was explained by the fact that a girl with a French officer, standing in the ruined Syrian Parliament, when spoken to by a correspondent, said with a toss of her head "Well this will teach them a lesson". This, rather sums up the French attitude.

Estimates today of the casualties in Damascus are as follows (though these figures cannot be confirmed at the moment): Syrian 500 to 600, French 60. In addition to the British major who lost his life in the Orient Palace, and who is reported to have called in the city on his way home on Python (special leave), a Church Army woman, who had valiantly decided to stay on when other British women were evacuated, was shot. She was going home shortly to have a baby.

Correspondents saw a pile of 60 bodies of Syrians lying in a courtyard, unable to be buried because the French were sweeping the streets with machineguns.

Staffs at the British Military hospital were operating continuously from 8:30 until 23:30 hours each day. A British hospital train—fortunately empty—was burnt out on Wednesday night at the Kanawat station. Though there was no loss of life, valuable equipment was destroyed. A dozen Syrian children, aged between seven and ten, were admitted to hospital with wounds. One boy of five had his hand shot off. Twenty or thirty women were also among the wounded. The maternity wing of the Syrian hospital was spattered with bullets fired from a house 50 yards away. A British army doctor who visited the place on June 1st—in the morning—found nine frightened women huddled in the basement, looked after by a couple of nurses. The hospital had previously been full, but the patients had run away when it became the object of attack.

Souks and mosques had been damaged by fire and bombs, and there had been cases of looting in the shops.

On the morning of June 1st, a French corporal was alleged by Syrians to have been found outside the Syrian hospital about to lob a grenade through the window. He was knocked down and shot with his own rifle. His body was brought to the British Military hospital, and the French were telephoned and ordered to take him away. In the man's pockets, were found parts of a clock and a large wad of money, but he had no identity papers. At first, the French refused to collect him, but when they did turn up after peremptory orders by a British officer, there were two loaded rifles in the French ambulance, which was marked with the Red Cross and FFL.

An officer told me he thought the whole affair had been deliberately organized by the local French forces as, before any actual firing occured, machine guns on the roofs of French buildings were trained on Syrian civilians.

This was Captain Letts's summary of the events, on the whole factually accurate, but quite obviously designed to influence public opinion against the French.

It was clear that all the British political officers in Syria were working to get the French out of Syria, and, as in 1943 in Lebanon, the French had fallen into the trap. De Gaulle's followers did just the thing they should have avoided—the use of their armed forces to try and squash any resistance ruthlessly. This policy had succeeded in the past when the world was interested in other things. But with the presence of correspondents in the area and the knowledge that the British would exploit the situation, they should have avoided such action.

No matter what Britain's motive might have been in aiding the Syrians, the Americans and British press on the whole praised their action, and the Moslem and Arab worlds hailed them as "liberators."

Immediately after, French troops and civilians began withdrawing from Damascus and other Syrian cities under the supervision of British soldiers, sailors, and marines. Befezzed Syrians, desert sheikhs, and tribesmen, their nationalistic spirit kindled to a fever pitch, jeered them on their way. As the French outward trek began, sullen crowds of Syrians, who had gathered from every section of the country, hissed and booed the long line of French infantrymen and trucks, tanks, and Bren gun carriers.

There were shouts of "Down with de Gaulle" and "Down with France." The French *poilus* glared back silently.

By contrast, the British naval party that came down from Beirut after disembarking from the cruiser *Arethusa* was cheered along the entire route from the Lebanese capital to Damascus. Headed by Comdr. C. E. Keys, the party included a marine band and scores of white-clad sailors and black-bereted Royal Marines.

There were the usual ceremonies, a march-past at the square in front of the Orient Palace by the Damascus-Hejaz railway station, and wildly cheering crowds, filled with enthusiasm and gratitude for the British who were putting on a dazzling show of smart soldiers, sailors, and marines.

It was in this same square that just over twenty years before, Colonel Stirling had watched King Feisal of Syria triumphantly entering Damascus, which was to be the capital of the United Arab Kingdom. Not much later, with the tacit agreement of Britain, France threw King Feisal out of Syria, and he received the kingdom of Iraq as a consolation prize.

Now, in that first day of June, Colonel Stirling was watching the French leave Syria, and a group of Syrian nationalists were taking over the reins. It was neither the pro-British Hashemite family nor another Arab monarch, but a young republic that was ridding itself of foreign influence. At the head of this state, was a man who had long fought for Arab freedom, Shukry Bey el Kuwatly, a tall, lean, hook-nosed man with a broad forehead.

I had never met the president of the Republic, but the time had come for an effort to see him and discuss the future of Syria, now that the French were out. President el Kuwatly was still in bed, suffering from his severe stomach ulcers. He was improving, however. Good news has great healing powers.

Thanks to Dudley Marsack, who was on excellent terms with the president, I managed to get to visit him. He was walking about in his room, and this was his first day out of bed. He was impatient to get out and about. His illness had left him somewhat short-tempered, and he was fingering his prayer beads agitatedly as he stalked about the place. When I asked him about what came next, he said: "This generation of Syrians will not tolerate seeing one Frenchman walk again through the streets of Damascus. I believe we are rid of France at last." His was a pure, undiluted hatred for anything French, a hatred which el Kuwatly and his followers were to pursue to somewhat ridiculous extremes in the first flush of victory.

In his deep, solemn voice, el Kuwatly categorically stated that France and Syria would never be able to get along together. "For twenty-five years, the Syrians and Lebanese have been living under a constant strain due to the presence of France. Now at last, because of their mad action, I believe we are rid of them. Now we can start improving our country, not basing ourselves on the whims of Frenchmen. There is much to be done, and we intend to call in American, British, and other experts to help and advise us."

The Syrian president grudgingly granted that diplomatic relations should be maintained with France but said that the French should henceforth be represented by a diplomatic representative like Spain, Sweden, and other nations, enjoying no special privileges. Neither would French businessmen be able to continue working in Syria at the expense of the local traders.

"They will have no communities in our towns unless there are among them people who wish to live in constant danger and risk of their lives every time they leave their houses," stormed the president.

"Syrians will not forget what they did to Damascus for another fifty years. The French must abandon hope of having strategic bases in the Levant."

El Kuwatly added, "Neither can they hope to keep their schools going in our country, because not one Syrian will want to have any contact with anything French. No father will send his sons or daughters to French schools." As he talked, he got more and more excited about the French. It was like a dam bursting. Here at long last, after years of waiting and manoeuvering, he could give full vent to his feelings.

"Do you realize that I," he said, thumping his chest, "that I, the president of Syria, have been sentenced to death by the French, three times in 1920, 1925, and 1927? Evidently, they forgot I was living on borrowed time as, each time, they suspended the execution indefinitely. They have killed, robbed, and humiliated us for twenty-five years. Now thanks to the Anglo-Americans, a bloody massacre and a long war in Syria have been prevented."

A few more polite exchanges, and the president shook hands with us. Officious attendants, anxious to impress all present by displaying an *exces de zèle*, ushered us out of the room.

Within a few days came the first reports of tribal clashes in the desert. The Syrians charged that French agents were behind it to prove to the world that Syrians could not run their own country alone. The French denied this charge but said that it was a typical trick in order to pave the way for further anti-French action in the country. But the days of France in the Levant were numbered, especially as an occupying power. After a few political huddles in which the newly formed United Nations and its Security Council faced one of the first tests, it was decided that all Allied Forces, both British and French and any other, would evacuate Syria and Lebanon.

French schools were closed down in Syria, but after a period where the country suffered from lack of enough educational institutions, they were reopened. Anything French was taboo for weeks after the shelling of Damascus. Syrians, especially those educated in French schools, had developed the habit of injecting a few French words into their Arabic conversation. "Bonjour," "merci," and a few other expressions were used automatically. But that was all "before." After the shelling, anybody using a

French word risked being beaten up. Even ''hallo,'' while answering the telephone, was considered French, and Syrians suddenly started saying ''hop hop,'' as an alternative. It sounded so silly to hear grown-ups suddenly saying quite seriously, ''hop hop,'' when they heard the telephone ring. All these were part of the transition fever. Within a few months, this exaggerated hatred of everything French had passed.

But the chain reaction of nationalism did not take long in spreading throughout the country. And with it came the excesses. With Palestine and the return of various elements whose activities had taken them to the Axis camp during the war, deep antiforeign feelings sprang up in Syria. The reaction to occupation by foreigners set in, and a wave of hatred emerged that was to affect the country. With the Palestine war Syria at first played a prominent role, only to fail dismally for a variety of reasons. These failures brought about a series of highly dramatic coups d'états and, in their wake, a period of insecurity.

XII
Egypt—Troubled Years

World War II had brought economic prosperity to Egypt, a lot of British troops, and a variety of problems that were to leave their mark on this country. During the war, tens of thousands of British, American, and Allied troops had converged on this land of the Pharaohs. In defeat, the Allies always fell back on Egypt. In victory, it was their springboard for attack.

The role of Egypt during the war has often been hotly debated. Some condemned her for not participating actively in the war and for leaving the defence of her own soil to others. One of the main reasons that Egypt had remained inactive was the fact that her army was unprepared and lacked any modern equipment. Britain had not given the Egyptian army any up-to-date weapons, and the British military missions had not properly trained the army. There were those who praised Egypt for abiding by the 1936 treaty of friendship and alliance with Britain, and for granting every facility to the Allied troops concentrated on her soil. Egypt had also severed diplomatic relations with the Axis nations. On the whole, most Allied political and military leaders claimed that Egypt had been reasonably loyal. In any case, many Egyptians did not consider the war their business.

The tens of thousands of Allied troops in the country enabled the leaders of Egypt to make money at an amazing rate. Soldiers spent their accumulated pay in the nightclubs of Cairo, buying souvenirs, sight-seeing, and enjoying the luxuries that an unrationed country could lay before their hungry eyes.

As the war receded from the frontiers of Egypt, and the fighting moved either westwards through North Africa into Europe or eastwards to the Orient, Egypt started having time to take stock of her new position. The war had left her richer than ever before. Prosperity had reached all classes, even the peasants, but, of course, it was mainly the upper classes that had benefited.

People who had lived modestly started splurging money in the manner of all nouveaux riches. Millionaires became multimillionaires. The effect of this wartime boom was only to be felt later, but it played a major role in the entry of communism into Egypt.

As the fighting developed elsewhere, many troops were shipped out, but Egypt had proved its worth as a base and remained a vital link between Europe and the Far East. There were still thousands of troops in the country and gigantic dumps of war equipment. The ports were always busy with naval and merchant marine traffic, while the airports, increased by scores of new fields, saw a steady, heavy traffic of planes. The presence of these foreign troops, especially the British, always a sore spot with the Egyptians, was to provoke troubles by the end of the war.

Much had been said during the critical war days to encourage the Middle Eastern countries to believe that with the end of the war would come the end of foreign occupation.

In 1943 the Lebanese, aided by the British for reasons of their own, had managed to get the upper hand over the occupying French. Definite promises to leave both Syria and Lebanon had been extracted.

The Egyptians, seeing their much smaller Arab neighbors getting such breaks and encouraged by the statements made during the war to them, hoped and believed that it would not be long before they would get rid of the British troops occupying their country and become completely free to rule themselves without interference from the British ambassador. Right through the war,

Lord Killearn, Britain's ambassador to Egypt, had meddled in Egyptian affairs. He had been heavy-handed and undiplomatic in his policy and foolishly and needlessly antagonized the Egyptians. More than ever, the Egyptians wanted to get rid of the British forces.

The excuse for British political interference in the war years was that they needed to get the utmost cooperation out of Egypt and could not take any risks by leaving matters entirely to the Egyptians. The British Embassy often brought pressure to bear on the Egyptians in their choice of government officials, in questions of policy, and other problems.

During the war, the Egyptian government had respected the terms of the 1936 treaty with Britain by granting bases, hospitals, food, and by complying with every request made by the military commanders. But while the government respected the Anglo-Egyptian treaty, there was little the government could do about the feelings of the Egyptian people about Britain.

The hatred grown of years of British occupation and the prewar struggle between the Egyptian nationalists and the British authorities could not be forgotten overnight by the people. Egyptians had struggled since the turn of the century to get rid of British domination. With the war, many nationalists thought that the salvation of the country might come through an Axis victory. Egypt was at that time subjected to an excellently organized propaganda campaign directed from both Italy and Germany, repeatedly telling the people that the Axis forces were coming as friends of the Egyptians to drive out the British and restore freedom to Egypt and the Arabs.

In view of the years-old antagonism between the nationalists and the British and the cleverly directed Axis propaganda, it was natural that there would be elements among the Egyptians who openly voiced their support of the Axis. With the military successes of the Germans, these Egyptian elements grew in number and started openly cheering the Axis in street demonstrations.

They hissed the British, celebrated every Axis victory, and waited for the Germans to enter Egypt.

The British embassy insisted that the government, then led by independent Hussein Sirry Pasha, take active steps to curb the anti-British feelings of the masses. Sirry Pasha, for this and other reasons resulting from British pressure, preferred to resign.

On February 4, 1942, the British committed one of their worst political blunders in Egypt. They decided that they would choose the next Egyptian cabinet and force it on King Farouk and his subjects. Lord Killearn, the British ambassador, always a domineering character who believed that tough tactics were best, bluntly delivered an ultimatum. The king must appoint Mustapha el Nahas as prime minister so that the popular Wafdist party would run the country.

He backed his ultimatum by British tanks and guns which surrounded Abdin Palace, the residence of the king. Should the young Egyptian monarch refuse, British troops would storm into the palace, conduct the king to a waiting plane where he would be taken to South Africa. With Killearn in the palace was General Stone, then commanding the British troops in Egypt. Stone was armed, and, outside, British tanks and guns had surrounded the palace.

It was not an easy decision for the proud king to make. Everything in him protested against this ultimatum. He would have preferred to be forcibly taken away rather than submit. He called in all the leading political leaders to consult them on the matter, but time was short. King Farouk knew that his refusal would mean much more than his just being forced out of throne and country. He felt that a bloody civil war could start. The people, especially prodded by the Axis, would fight a losing war against the British.

The king consented to accept Nahas Pasha's cabinet, and the British ambassador withdrew, taking with him his tanks and guns. The whole incident was to leave a bitter mark on all Egyptians, and even those who were ardently pro-British found it hard to stomach. There were other more diplomatic and subtle ways that the British could have used. They chose what might have been the quickest, but certainly not the wisest, way. More than ever before, the Egyptians were determined to get rid of the British military occupation of their country.

Despite this, the Egyptians carried on with their obligations as required by the Anglo-Egyptian treaty. In the summer of 1942, the British forces in the western desert were in a bad situation. Field Marshal Rommel was advancing to the gates of Alexandria. The Egyptian cabinet met for ten hours, one of their longest meetings, to discuss the situation and reach a series of decisions designed to aid the British and Allied forces.

For example, Sharia el Malika, or Queen's Street, was closed to all civilian traffic between eight in the morning to midnight in order to allow the uninterrupted flow of Allied reinforcements being rushed to the Western Desert. These forces were being brought from India and the Far East and rushed from Suez to Cairo, and from there to the Western Desert by train. Sharia el Malika linked the Suez road to the main railway station.

The government also arrested all potential troublemakers and anti-Allied suspects, deporting them to El Tor camp in the southern part of the Sinai peninsula in order to make sure they did not start any sabotage against the British.

The Egyptian army was called into Cairo and Alexandria to ensure security, and guard bridges and public utilities against any attempt at sabotage. Egyptian soldiers, armed, were stationed everywhere and thus relieved the British soldiers, badly needed elsewhere. To the extent that the Egyptians had arms, and within the limits of their sadly incomplete training, they did their best for the Allied cause at this most critical time. The British were surprised by this respect for the treaty and the way the Egyptians cooperated. Winston Churchill and various other Allied leaders publicly praised Egypt's stand at that time.

About two months later, Montgomery launched his famous offensive from El Alamein which drove back the Axis forces out of Egypt and kept them retreating through North Africa. On November 8, American and British troops landed in North Africa, and the continent was soon completely rid of the Axis.

The war had shown that Egypt was indeed the gateway to Asia and the meeting place of three continents. Its importance had grown, and both military strategists and politicians predicted that in future years Egypt's role would be even greater in world affairs.

With the tide of war receding from Africa and the Middle East, Britain's interference in local affairs diminished. The excuse was gone, and gradually, the British started realizing that times were changing. Egyptians no longer meekly submitted to the dictation of others. They had seen other smaller nations come to enjoy full sovereignty and independence and did not see why they had to blindly obey the directives of the British ambassador.

On October 8, 1944, King Farouk decided to dismiss Nahas Pasha and his cabinet and entrusted the formation of the new ministry to Ahmed Maher Pasha, leader of the Saadist party. Maher Pasha formed a cabinet which included members of his party, the Liberal-Constitutionals, the Kotla (dissident Wafdists), and Nationalists.

The victorious Allies were already laying the foundations of peace and had informed Egypt and other nations that had sided with them, but had not participated in the war actively, that the time had come for them to declare war on the Axis. The reason for this was to enable them become members of the United Nations Organization whose foundation would soon be laid in San Francisco.

Maher Pasha had personally believed that Egypt should have entered the war a long time back and had said so. But the popular feeling in Egypt was that there was no reason for Egyptians to die in order to defend a British Empire whose very tenet was to prevent Egypt from gaining her independence. Now there was the question of declaring war in order to join an international body whose membership would provide great political prestige and advantages.

Even then, the Egyptian prime minister felt he could not undertake such a step without consulting all leaders. Because of the critical times through which the country was passing, Maher Pasha had formed a consultative group including all the elder statesmen of the country, the prominent personalities who, while perhaps having no political party behind them, had a right to express their opinion in the crucial moments of Egypt's life.

So Maher Pasha summoned them to a meeting where he exposed the problem. He knew that any such declaration of war would be bitterly attacked by the masses, for without doubt a good proportion of the young nationalists were definitely against siding with Britain even at that stage. However, in view of Maher Pasha's explanations that the reason for declaring war was solely intended to allow Egypt to join the United Nations, the elder statesmen approved the idea.

In turn, the cabinet agreed that the Egyptian government should declare war on the Axis. They did not envy Maher Pasha his task of explaining this matter either to Parliament or to the masses, especially the students whose anti-British sentiments were notorious. But Maher had previously shown he knew how to handle the students. When they demonstrated and threatened public security, he had personally driven up to the university unescorted and addressed them. Despite his short stature and his portliness, his voice and his courage had won him the respect of the youthful mobs.

Maher Pasha invited the student council to tea to explain the situation to them. He had faith in the coming generation. While others had either used the students to promote their own needs by spurring them to riots, often priming them with money and misleading information, Maher Pasha considered them worthy of his respect and consideration. He outlined the situation to the students and they understood his views. They did not hide from him their distrust of Britain and frankly said they suspected this of being another treacherous British move. In the long run, Maher Pasha carried the day and the students were assured that the declaration of war would not mean that Egyptians were to be sent as cannon fodder to the Far East, a rumor that had been spreading. It would be a defensive declaration of war, designed purely to enable Egypt to join the United Nations.

Next, Maher had to convince the Parliament. The question was an open secret. The same thing was happening elsewhere. Rumors spread throughout the streets that the Allies were forcing Egypt into the war because they estimated they would need millions of men to invade the islands of Japan. They would wear down Japanese resistance by sending Turks, Arabs, Indians, and other soldiers to do the dirty work, and then they would follow for the kill. This was the propaganda, and there were many among the masses who believed it.

On February 22, Maher Pasha summoned secret sessions of both houses of Parliament—the Chamber of Deputies and the Senate. He addressed the deputies first and outlined the matter to them in detail. Nationalist party member Fikri Abaza, prominent writer and editor in chief of the weekly magazine, *Al Mussawar*, opposed Maher Pasha's viewpoint and took the attitude that Egypt should not declare war. The debate lengthened and Maher, remembering that the Senate was waiting for him, decided to walk over to the upper house to ask the senators to wait for him.

The two houses are linked by a passage leading to the Pharaonic Hall. As Maher reached the hall, a youth shot him four times. Maher Pasha died almost immediately. His bodyguard arrested the young man, El Issawi.

That night, at about midnight, Mahmoud Fahmy el Nokrashy Pasha, Maher's right-hand man, became the leader of the Saadist party and succeeded the murdered man as prime minister.

An investigation showed that El Issawi did not seem connected to any political party. He was spurred on by his own ideas of what would happen if Egypt declared war. He had listened to the whispering campaign and had become convinced that Maher Pasha was driving Egypt to her doom, and that thousands of young men would be conscripted to fight for the hated British.

Time was pressing, and on February 25, Parliament approved the declaration of war against the Axis, and Egypt's name was included on the list of those nations that were to become the founder members of the United Nations.

The time came for Egypt to revise her problems. In March 1945, the Egyptian government asked Britain to start negotiations designed to bring about the realization of Egypt's national aspirations. The United Kingdom expressed its readiness to negotiate to revise the old 1936 treaty.

Egypt wanted the complete evacuation of all British troops from Egyptian soil and the unification of Egypt and the Sudan under the Egyptian crown. The public was pressing for this and the powerful Wafdist party, now forming the opposition, continually hammered at this point. The Wafdists prodded students and other groups to demonstrate in favour of the British leaving the country. Nokrashy's government had no alternative but to show the masses that they were not puppets of the British but were sincerely determined to get the British to leave Egypt.

Thus even though the Egyptian government had several post-war problems on its hands, Nokrashy Pasha pressed for an immediate revision of the 1936 treaty. During the war, there had been no question of the British forces abandoning the vital bases of Egypt, but now the Egyptians wanted them to leave. The British, on the other hand, said that a treaty existed that remained good until 1956 and saw no reason for completely evacuating the country. There were possible compromise solutions, said the British, and that was why they were accepting to hold a conference to study the revision of the treaty.

As far as the Sudan was concerned, the British seemed more determined than ever to hold on to it. Technically, the Anglo-Egyptian Sudan was a condominium, supposed to be jointly ruled by the British and the Egyptians. In fact, the Egyptians had little or nothing to say in the entire matter. The flags of both Britain and Egypt fluttered over the governor-general's palace, but inside the palace, sat an English governor-general, again technically approved by the king of Egypt. His secretaries were all British. There were a few minor Egyptian officials in the country, but the key jobs and policymakers were all held by British.

The then British minister of state, Lord Stansgate, came out with a delegation to discuss the matter with the Egyptians. The Cairo government formally demanded the evacuation of British troops and unity of the Sudan. The British countered by offering to revise the 1936 treaty but pointed out that they had no intention of completely abandoning their military bases in Egypt.

Another problem had then cropped out, a problem that had existed for a long time but had never enflamed the Egyptians before—Palestine. The Egyptians had become interested in Arab problems since 1943 when the Lebanese fought the French. This interest grew after the formation of the Arab League in 1944, and the Egyptians started taking a keen interest in the Holy Land. True, they had not yet reached the stage where the question of Palestine excluded all others, as was the case with Iraq, but it was a problem they now considered as much their own as the question of the Sudan.

During the war, the Arab struggle for Palestine had lain dormant, and there had been little contact between the exiled leaders, particularly Haj Amin el Husseini, the grand mufti of Jerusalem, and their people. Now there were various Palestinian and other leaders starting to stir again, and from Cairo, the first rumbles could be heard. In Palestine itself, the Arab people remained quiet. It was the Jewish element that, for some time, had been striking at the British and organizing terrorist groups. The Jewish threat was starting to make itself felt, both to the British, who were smarting under their blows, and to the Arabs, who felt uneasy at the normally docile Jew swinging into action.

At the same time in Egypt, a powerful, popular group suddenly emerged to challenge the established political parties. This was the Muslim Brotherhood. It had started some time back as a small religious organization but had become a large group that now entered the political field. Unlike the other political parties of Egypt, it had a program as well as a popular leader. This program broadly consisted of a return to Islam and the Koranic law, and to achieve this, the members felt that they must crush all foreign influence, which they considered stood in the way of their ultimate object.

The Muslim Brotherhood held an undeniable popular appeal. The Egyptian masses are on the whole very devout Muslims. The Brotherhood attracted them by directing their religious fervor into the political field. While the other parties consisted mainly of loyal followers owing allegiance to a leader, irrespective of his political program or lack thereof, the Muslim Brotherhood had definite emotional appeal.

Their leader was a short, bearded man called Sheikh Hassan el Banna. He was not much to look at, wore shabby European clothes, topped by a red tarboush. But he hypnotized the masses. He could speak with a soft, mild voice that caressed the people and filled them with religious fervor. He could also roar out inflammatory speeches to whip the masses into action.

It was against this background that the first Anglo-Egyptian talks to be held after World War II started. Nationalism and Arabism complemented each other to create a hatred for the foreigners and a determination to get rid of the British, by bloodshed and violence if need be. The political parties, those in and out of power and not to be outdone by each other, preached the same gospel.

Rioting started throughout Egypt. The Muslim Brotherhood swung into action in Cairo and Alexandria, demonstrating, clashing with the police, smashing public utilities, lampposts, and window shops, and demanding the immediate expulsion of the British from the Egyptian soil.

Not to be outdone, the other popular party, the Wafdists, also demonstrated, clashed with the police, and rioted. They, too, demanded the evacuation of the British and the realisation of Egyptian aspirations. Nahas Pasha, the man who was placed in power by the British in 1942, now demanded that the government get rid of the British. At the same time, he claimed that any negotiations at which the Wafidists were not present would not commit his party, the biggest in the country.

It was not only for Egypt that the Egyptians were demonstrating. It was for Palestine. On November 3, 1945, for example, leaders of the masses called for a general strike to protest against the Balfour Declaration, which had promised the Zionists a national home in Palestine. Shops, both Egyptian and foreign, were closed, and all institutions shut down for the day. Many people stayed home and waited for the storm that would inevitably come.

In many parts of Cairo and Alexandria, groups of looters smashed shops and clashed with the police. Many people were hurt in the streets. In Alexandria especially, there was considerable bloodshed. Six people were killed, 146 wounded. The police arrested 417 rioters and looters.

At that time, too, the authorities noticed that a few communist elements had appeared among the rioting masses. These communists were united with other dissidents to create difficulties for the regime and to protest against British policy in Egypt and in Palestine. Nokrashy Pasha had a very difficult time. His coalition cabinet grouped four parties that did not have the popular backing of either the Wafdists or the Muslim Brotherhood.

To have to fight the two together was a tough job, but backed by the army and the police, he could hold them in check.

His methods were, perhaps necessarily, brutal. Nokrashy Pasha was himself a mild, pleasant man who in his younger days had also been a student leader, agitating for much the same thing that those students were clamoring for in 1945. But he could not let the situation get out of hand.

I went to watch a typical riot, which started off by a meeting in the gardens of the Fuad el Awal University at Giza, on the route of the famed pyramids. There, various students were lifted on the shoulders of their colleagues to address the crowds of young men and women who had left their classrooms. Little academic work had been done that year.

The speeches were fiery, denouncing the weak government, the perfidious British, and urging the students to take the law into their own hands. Among the speakers were some who were completely unknown to the students. One claimed he was a colleague from Alexandria, another from Assiout. There was little doubt that they were communist agitators, but the students did not mind. They were willing to listen to anybody who told them to riot against Britain.

After one hour of speeches, the students rolled out of the campus grounds, heading towards the Nile. They wanted to cross the bridges, get to the other side to join other demonstrators, and march on the British Embassy and the business part of the city. As they marched, they broke branches off the trees and armed themselves as well as they could.

At the end of the avenue leading to the university stood a solid line of steel-helmeted policemen, armed mainly with staves and some with rifles. There were reinforcements hidden and still others in lorries waiting to rush to whatever point that might weaken under the weight of thousands of students. The youths divided themselves into groups, some marching down the main avenue, others taking the side streets in the hope that they might find a loophole in the cordons around the university area. But the police had sealed every road that led from the university to the Nile.

I marched behind those that took the main avenue. As they came within hailing distance of the police, they stopped, shouted a few slogans and started throwing stones at the police. The policemen raised their left arms, to which they had attached shields, and warded off most of the stones. A few men were slightly hurt. Then they charged, their staves working like flails, smashing down students to the ground. The poorly organized youths melted before the expert charges of the policemen, and they started running in every direction. Here and there, a small group battled grimly against the police, but they were gradually overpowered and marched off to waiting trucks.

The policemen, angry and overexcited, would continue beating the students even after they had surrendered, bruised and bleeding.

I managed to dodge the police, who thought I was also a student, and walked to the edge of the Nile where several students had managed to arrive despite the barricades. As they knew the bridges were guarded by other strong forces, they made for some waiting sailing boats that would ferry them across the river to join the other demonstrators.

They piled into the feluccas and started feverishly trying to get the big, sluggish boats into the stream. Mounted steel-helmeted policemen clattered up, dismounted, and started throwing stones into the boats that were a few feet away just below the embankment. They lifted heavy boulders and sent them hurtling down on the students. The rocks tore holes in the boats and badly hurt the students. A few boats quickly surrendered, and as more policemen rushed up, the others saw it would be impossible to make their crossing.

A police officer yelled to them that even if they escaped the stones, he would order his men to open fire. The students returned to the shore where the panting policemen hauled them out of the boats, shoved them through a gauntlet of their stave-swinging comrades until the beaten and bleeding youths reached the waiting lorries that were taking them to jail. From the nearby Turkish and Lebanese legations, diplomats were yelling at the police to calm down and stop beating the students who had surrendered, but they turned a deaf ear to their pleas. Those boys got cruel treatment that day.

A few days later, a similar incident occured, only this time with more serious repercussions. It had become known in Egypt as the Abbas Bridge incident. Again the students rushed out of the university, trying to make for the heart of Cairo across the Abbas Bridge. They met little resistance from the police and, triumphantly charging, they found themselves on the bridge. At that moment, the bridge started swinging open and they found themselves looking down at the swiftly flowing river. They looked behind them and found that a very strong force of police had suddenly appeared from their hiding places and were blocking their retreat.

Slowly, the policemen advanced, shields thrust forward, staves ready to strike. Then they pounced on the students. It was a furious battle, but very one-sided. Again the students got a bad beating. In fact, it was a worse beating than ever before. Many, to escape the merciless pounding, were jumping into the Nile. Others were thrown in by the fighting policemen. Several died, drowned in the Nile. The government denied all this, but there were even some government members that felt that this was inhuman treatment of misguided youths.

In any case, the opposition was getting too strong for the government, and this decided Makram Ebeid Pasha to resign from the cabinet and withdraw his party from the coalition. Nokrashy Pasha was forced to quit.

The king asked a tough old politician to head the next coalition cabinet. Ismail Sidky Pasha, independent financial wizard, feared, hated but respected, stepped into the breach. Sidky Pasha was generally considered one of the most outspoken, forthright politicians. He brooked no nonsense when he was in power but could be practical and reasonable. He was a businessman with his own political ideas. He feared no one and no party. In the past, he had dismissed Parliament and ruled by an iron hand. When the popular Wafdists had tried to block him, he had outwitted them. Once, when he did not want Nahas Pasha to deliver an election speech in the provinces, he had his railway coach diverted from the main line to one that led to a point in the desert several miles from nowhere and just left him there for a while. He believed that Egypt should have an agreement with Britain and was known to admire the Jews. He said so himself and scorned the bitter attacks that were showered on him by his countrymen and other Arabs.

He stepped in, and people promptly expected a new situation. They were not disappointed.

Sidky Pasha formed a cabinet consisting of Saadists, Liberal Constitutionals, and Nationalists under his independent, nonpartisan leadership. From the start, he adopted a policy completely different to his predecessors in handling the rioting students and the Muslim Brotherhood. Although he had always believed in having an agreement with Britain, he publicly stated he was against the continued occupation of Egypt by British troops.

He pointed out to the masses that it was silly for them to clash with Egyptian government troops. These forces, he argued, represented people whose aims were identical to those of the students. But the authorities were for law and order, and to prove that he supported the ideas of the students and other demonstrators, he placed himself at the head of a demonstration and marched to a protest meeting against the continued presence of British troops in Egypt. Sidky Pasha merely insisted that these demonstrations be peaceful. They should neither break lampposts, which were Egyptian property, nor shops. Neither should they attack the British Embassy, Consulate, or military installations. It was by negotiations that two civilized nations could reach an agreement, he said.

But this state of affairs did not suit some elements among the rioters whose main aim seemed to be not so much the expulsion of the British from the country as the upsetting of any stability in Cairo. It did not take them long to transform subsequent demonstrations into riots, during which shop windows were again smashed, lampposts shattered, trolleys overturned and burned, resulting in an inevitable clash with the Egyptian police.

One riot went further. The Egyptian masses headed for Kasr el Nil Barracks, one of the principal British military garrisons in Cairo. Kasr el Nil barracks were situated near the world famous Egyptian Museum, home of the finest Pharaonic treasures to have been unearthed during decades of archeological excavations in the deserts of Egypt. A howling mass of youths charged headlong towards the sentries guarding the barbed wire entrance. The British guards fired into the crowds, killing one Egyptian and wounding several others. The masses retired, then charged again, trying to set fire to the British depots. Finally, they were forced to withdraw.

There were other similar incidents. Masses tried to attack British installations in various parts of Cairo. Once, they charged a poorly defended house in which women auxiliary forces were quartered. The sentries at the gates kept the crowd at bay, until a force of British tanks and armored cars rushed up from the nearby Kasr el Nil barracks and surrounded the area, keeping the growing crowds away. This was the first time since the rioting started that the British took the law into their own hands rather than rely on the Egyptian police to handle the masses, but there had been no time to lose. To await the arrival of the slower police force might have provoked a massacre of the British girls in the house.

The British Embassy, still headed by Lord Killearn, had shown little astuteness in handling the Egyptian case so far. At the end of the war, the British should have had the intelligence to remove their troops from the Egyptian cities of Cairo and Alexandria at least. During the war, the people had accepted the British, and indeed, many were glad to see them around. With the peace, people started growing impatient at seeing drunken Tommies aggressively demanding money for more drinks from civilians and many such incidents that inevitably arise from any army occupying towns. And the Union Jack flying over buildings that dominated the city just maddened the nationalists.

Lord Killearn should have realized that this situation would inevitably give way to the Egyptians demanding the evacuation of British troops. It would have been more graceful for the British to pull out their troops from Cairo and Alexandria before such a demand came through. More than that, it would have been a gesture of good will that might have averted much trouble later. Many of Killearn's assistants, and even several of the senior British military officers, had openly told the British ambassador that it might be a good idea to evacuate the cities before the Egyptians thought of demanding it. The British would thus show the Egyptians that they were considerate and sympathetic to their national aspirations, and this might have averted the Egyptians asking for the immediate evacuation of the British from the Suez Canal zone as well.

Killearn refused to consider such action. He firmly believed in putting up a show of force, of waving the flag. Unfortunately, Killearn was some years behind his times.

The result was that the Egyptians did start demanding that the British troops leave both the cities and the Suez Canal zone as well. The fact that the British maintained their large-sized garrisons in Cairo and Alexandria made them suspicious and resentful, and the attitude of the British ambassador was incomprehensible to a nation seeking its independence. Thus, the demonstrations and the rioting grew, and the agitators found willing volunteers among the young men and the workers. It was the chance of a lifetime for various extremist elements to win popular support. The Muslim Brotherhood made the most of the situation, and so did the communists.

The Reds won many converts among the youths, both the industrial workers and university students. It would be grossly unfair to say that the attitude of the British ambassador was the main reason for the growth of communism in Egypt, but certainly the situation created by the continued presence of British troops aided communist agitators to win a good measure of public support.

The rioting and demonstrations, no longer peaceful but directed against both the British and the Egyptian authorities, gave Sidky Pasha the excuse he was seeking to ban any demonstrations whatsoever. From having marched at their head at the beginning, he now forbade any gatherings and did not even accept to allow peaceful demonstrations through the streets.

This law was not to the liking of the Muslim Brotherhood, who from that moment fought Sidky Pasha and allied themselves to all those who opposed him.

While all this was happening, negotiations between the British and the Egyptians continued. Lord Stansgate and his British team were in constant conference with the Egyptians. Sidky Pasha had decided that not only the cabinet, but also the Elder Statesmen's Council formed by Maher Pasha would attend the negotiations. Only the Wafdists stayed out. Their viewpoint was that they represented the majority of the people, and therefore, they, as the rightful ambassadors of the Egyptians, should head the delegation.

Even then, the majority of the Egyptian elder statesmen and, indeed, many of the cabinet members, opposed Sidky Pasha's viewpoint. The British delegation had put forward a scheme to replace the Anglo-Egyptian treaty and the presence of an independent British force on Egyptian soil. It had wanted to create a joint defense agreement whereby a united Anglo-Egyptian force, under a mixed military commission, would be responsible for the defense of the Suez Canal zone. Thus, instead of having an independent British force, the soldiers of the two nations would join together. Egypt's sensitivity would thus be satisfied and the nation would get the feeling that it was sharing, with an ally on an equal footing, the burdens of defence.

Sidky Pasha fully approved this plan. He had always felt that at the present stage of their national development, the Egyptians alone could not possibly handle the defence of the Suez Canal. Neither could Egypt afford it. Always more of a realist driven by logic rather than a nationalist fired by passion, Sidky Pasha considered joint defence as the best solution for the time being.

Most of his colleagues of the Egyptian delegation did not see eye to eye with him. Several stated that even if the joint defence commission consisted of an equal number of British and Egyptian officers, the commission would undoubtedly be run by the technically superior British officers. They felt that the Egyptians would be no more than stooges and decided that they could not trust Britain's intentions in proposing such a plan. They had no other plan to put forward short of the complete, unconditional evacuation of the British forces, a plan which the British felt they could not consider, even though the Egyptian delegation hinted that once the evacuation was completed, then Egypt, of its own free will, would reach a satisfactory agreement with the British.

Sidky Pasha was convinced that the plan would serve the best interests of Egypt and help protect the country from the dangers of a sudden Russian invasion. He felt that the majority of the delegation was being unrealistic, and in the case of many of his colleagues, they were speaking for the gallery and the masses rather than in the highest interest of the country. He admitted that some were prompted by a genuine distrust of the British.

On the whole, however, he was sure that those who opposed him were shortsighted and narrow-minded. So sure was he of the need for such a joint defence commission, that he was prepared to carry it through on his own personal responsibility. Sidky Pasha had always been used to making firm decisions, whether in politics or in business, and he never relished the idea of having to consult others. So, he packed his bags and set off by plane to London where he felt he could work unhampered by the elder statesmen and other politicians. His only assistant was Ibrahim Abdul Hadi Pasha, the minister of foreign affairs in his cabinet, who later was to play an important and thankless role in the life of Egypt.

Within one week Sidky Pasha returned from London with an agreement in principle that was to be known as the Bevin-Sidky project. He called a secret session of Parliament and outlined the proposed project in detail. Parliament approved, but the details were not made public.

In the project, the British evacuation would take place by October 1949 from all of Egypt. Some kind of military agreement would have been drawn up between the two nations so that at least a combined staff would be formed to organize the defence of the Suez Canal. But no British forces would remain in the country. Sidky also announced that he had won for Egypt sovereignty over the Sudan. This announcement was made public.

Immediately after it was announced, the governor-general of the Sudan, Sir Robert Howe, proclaimed that this was not true. From London the then foreign secretary, Ernest Bevin, described Sidky's statement as "misleading."

In strongly worded terms, Sidky Pasha attacked the governor-general of the Sudan. He charged him with meddling in affairs that were beyond his competence. The governor-general, always an Englishman but appointed with the approval of the king of Egypt according to the 1899 agreement on the Sudan, rules from a palace that flies both the Union Jack and the Egyptian flag. He is supposed to be a servant of both these countries, administering an area of which both nations were supposed to be partners.

The problem of the Sudan was certainly a delicate one, with several views submitted by various sides. But one thing was definite—as the servant of both Britain and Egypt, it was certainly not the business of the governor-general to contradict the statements of one of his employers. It showed that no matter what the Egyptians did, in point of fact, the British were violating the terms and spirit of the agreement by running the Sudan as if it was a British colony.

The Sudanese problem consisted mainly of three main parts. The Egyptians wanted to proclaim the "unity of the Nile Valley" and definitely bring the Sudan under the throne of Egypt. They hastened to emphasize that the Sudan would not be a colony, but a partner. It would have its own parliament and its autonomous regime, but always under the Egyptian crown. The Nile, that great provider to both countries, was reason enough for such unity, but other things also united them they claimed. They also shared the same religion, had a common past, and spoke the same language.

The British did not agree with this view. They said that the Sudan was entirely different from Egypt, and the people had little in common with the Egyptians. They claimed the Sudanese did not want to become part of Egypt and that they preferred having the British help them reach independence in slow but sure stages.

The opinion of the Sudanese also varied. Some wanted to be united to Egypt, others wanted to remain under British rule, at least for the time being. Still others wanted to become independent and have their own king or leader. It was difficult to gauge the strength of each group, but in any case, all these vociferous groups could only represent small portions of the population of five to six million inhabitants.

The storm that was created by the Sidky statement on the Sudan, followed as it was by a denial from the governor-general and Bevin's refutation, caused the collapse of the Sidky regime in Egypt. He had committed himself to reaching an agreement with the British government, and when he came back with a project he could not push through, he was discredited by the British. Had this agreement gone through, the British troops would have been out of Egypt in 1949, and considerable trouble might have been averted.

The new Egyptian premier, Mahmoud el Nokrashy Pasha, decided to break off the direct talks with Britain and submit the Anglo-Egyptian deadlock to the Security Council of the United Nations. He convened both houses of Parliament.

Parliament was packed that night, and King Farouk came as a private individual, incognito, to listen to the dramatic announcement. For the first time Egypt would seek international arbitration against Britain, whereas previously matters had always been decided by direct negotiations. As he sat in the visitors' gallery, King Farouk was recognized by the deputies and cheered long and loud.

Nokrashy Pasha, as expected, announced that the talks with the British had broken down and that he was going to take the case to the Security Council. The debates were loud and furious, and there were several startling interruptions when Egyptian youths, sitting in the visitors' galleries, shouted anti-British slogans and delivered impromptu speeches before they were bounced out. The Egyptian premier maintained that the presence of the British in Egypt was a grave menace to international security as it would provoke a tense situation that might lead to trouble.

The final result turned out that the Security Council did not want to pass judgement on that case. The two sides were advised to continue their direct negotiations, but the dispute was kept on the Security Council agenda. The problem was once again back in the laps of the British and the Egyptians, and the deadlock continued. There was nothing that the Egyptian delegation, headed by Premier Nokrashy Pasha himself, could do to force a decision by the Security Counil.

Nokrashy Pasha returned with a general policy to ignore the British in the Suez Canal zone. There was little else he could do. He had tried negotiations, and he had gone to the United Nations. In both instances he had met with little success, and now he decided to maintain a dignified silence. He felt he had much to do inside the country, and he started on a program of social reforms and plans to strengthen the hitherto neglected Egyptian army.

This policy was designed to make up for years of neglect in internal reforms, which had advanced very slowly. As for the army, such plans were long overdue. At the expense of internal reforms, the Egyptian government had always been struggling to get rid of the British and concentrating on their foreign affairs problems. As far as the army was concerned, so long as the British had been in the country, they had decided to restrict the Egyptian forces to about forty thousand troops with little training in the modern methods of warfare.

While many of the Egyptians' arguments against the continued British occupation of Egypt were quite justified, they could not honestly refute the British charge that the Egyptians alone were not capable of defending the Suez Canal zone. Although Egyptian leaders asserted strongly that their forces could defend the Canal, it was obvious to all trained observers that they were not equipped or trained to ward off an attack by even a small nation, let alone a world power. However, their army had been restricted by British policy, which had ruled them for years, and there was no need to feel ashamed of their poor military standing. However, it was time to modernize and expand their forces.

As it turned out, Nokrashy Pasha was unable to implement any constructive plans. Demonstrations continued throughout the country, and real acts of terrorism started. Grenades and bombs were thrown at the legations of those countries that had not supported Egypt during the Security Council debates.

The situation was very tense throughout Egypt, and the people were very impatient at the sight of British troops still moving around the streets. The war had ended, and many resented the continued housing shortage, the high cost of living, and occasional fights among the Tommies and Egyptians. Occupation forces of any army in the world often tend to antagonize civilians, and the British forces were by no means an exception to this general rule.

The British started to realize what they should have realized years earlier—that it was high time they evacuated at least the cities of Cairo and Alexandria. Their most aggressive opponents were in those two areas and consisted mainly of students and workers. By evacuating these two towns, they would placate to some extent the feeling of the Egyptian nationalists. So gradually, and as gracefully as possible, the British troops were withdrawn from barracks they had occupied on some pretext or other for the past sixty years.

The historic citadel dominating Cairo was handed over to the Egyptians. King Farouk went there and hoisted an Egyptian flag to replace the Union Jack that had so annoyed the Egyptians. Local forces were stationed in the barracks. The famous Kasr el Nil barracks were also handed over to the Egyptians amid the joy and festivity of the nationalists. The English naval bases in Alexandria were withdrawn, and British troops that had for long concentrated in various key garrisons throughout the two biggest cities of Egypt vanished.

The British headed for the Suez Canal zone, which became their area of concentration. At Fayed, an obscure village near Ismailia on the Bitter Lakes, German prisoners of war built the new headquarters for the British Middle East forces.

At long last, the British government thought fit to remove Lord Killearn, and in his place came Sir Ronald Campbell, a smiling, pleasant diplomat. In the place of the domineering, arrogant giant, who looked down on the Egyptians from his six-foot-plus frame, came a quiet little man who spoke calmly to the Egyptians in tones they did not resent.

He came at a bad time and had a thankless, impossible job of reconciling his government's viewpoint and that of the Egyptians. He did not succeed, but nevertheless gained the respect and genuine liking of the local leaders.

As 1947 wore on and 1948 loomed ahead, the local situation became even gloomier. People started becoming aware of the Palestine situation. Egypt's interest in the Holy Land was growing, and whipped by religious, nationalist, and pan-Arab leaders, this zeal for Palestine mushroomed during the next few months.

Throughout the Arab countries, the people were preparing for war against the Zionists and their sympathizers. Not to be outdone, Egypt's leaders called on the people to prepare to struggle for the liberation of the Holy Land and to protect its Arab population. Among those who championed the "Jihad" or Holy War for Palestine was the Muslim Brotherhood. In the name of Palestine, they started collecting arms, and were not opposed by the authorities.

Terrorism was rampant. A mine was placed in the Jewish quarter of Cairo, and its explosion killed nine and wounded many. There were bombs and jeep loads of TNT that exploded at Cicurel's, Cairo's Jewish-owned department store; at the Société Orientale de Publicité, a British-owned but Jewish-managed publishing firm; at the Ades building, and at other Jewish stores in the city. Bombs exploded at the Metro cinema and other halls showing MGM films.

The situation was very ugly and, for a while, it seemed that the police were either powerless or unwilling to intervene. It was no longer safe for fair-haired, white-skinned people to walk through the streets of Cairo, especially beyond the centre of the town. Anybody with a camera was suspected of being a Jewish spy. An American tourist, David Haas, was stoned to death near the bazaars. A French boxing coach, hired to train the Egyptian national team, was beaten to death by a mob in the heart of the city.

There were amazing situations. They did not mean that all the nation was out chasing foreigners and Jews through the city, but there were enough mobs formed to cause serious trouble. Amid the drama there were some amusing incidents to record. One day, an Egyptian Muslim youth, very fair-haired and easily able to pass for a foreigner, was walking with his dark-skinned Jewish friend. A howling mob rushed down the street, surrounded the two friends, and set about beating the fair-haired Muslim. The dark-skinned Jew was untouched. The Jew rushed into the mob, shoving them away from his Muslim friend, and yelled at them, ''Don't beat him. I swear to you he is a Muslim,'' and then cautiously added, ''like me.'' The crowd let them alone and swirled away, seeking other victims.

There were days of terror in which the masses, whipped by the double-barrelled threats of the Egyptian and Palestinian crises, made Cairo and Alexandria two very unhealthy spots. The hatred of the masses had infiltrated into the junior ranks of government officials, and foreigners had a really tough time. The occasional tourist stopping off in Cairo was subjected to every type of rudeness and red tape imaginable by police officers, passport control, and customs officials. Some people were forced to strip naked, other had their bags upended and subjected to every sort of humiliation.

For a few weeks Egypt was in a hysterical, fanatical mood, and tourists and other foreigners returned home to give a terrible picture of the country. For years after, the tourist trade of Egypt, usually very flourishing in winter, suffered because of those few weeks. People had not realized that this had been a passing phase and that shortly after, Egyptian officials wore their best smiles for visitors and that tourists were made welcome and every facility given them.

This period created a series of complications for the Egyptian government. Foreign diplomats kept coming to see Premier Nokrashy Pasha with notes of protest because their nationals were being beaten up.

There was talk of the British army marching from the Suez Canal zone bases to occupy Cairo and Alexandria unless the Egyptian authorities proved able to cope with the rioters and protect nationals and foreigners alike from the fury of the crowds. The police were active and about eight hundred Muslim Brethren and suspected communists were interned, but there was nothing that the authorities could do to prevent further bloodshed.

In fact, the rioting increased as the Arabs felt that the United Nations and the world in general backed the Zionists to the detriment of the Arabs. This, perhaps more than any other single factor, created a hatred for all foreigners. The Egyptians did not know why the outside world had turned against them. They accused the United States in particular of being under the influence of the Jewish bankers and President Truman of being a puppet in the hands of his Jewish advisers. They felt that their case was being totally ignored in the world's press and that only the Jewish side of the story was being told. The Arabs, of course, did not realize that they were totally lacking in public relations men whose job it would have been to present the Arab case intelligently to world public opinion.

Right or wrong, they were in an ugly mood, and stirred by those who purpose was served by sowing chaos in the land, they rioted, striking blindly, furiously, and often with no more than superficial results against innocent victims.

In December 1948, there was a big riot at the Faculty of Medicine. As was customary, the students were in the forefront of the fighting. By now it was commonly said that the students were on the whole divided into two main camps, those who had joined the Muslim Brotherhood and those who were members of communist cells. The Faculty of Medicine riot developed into a bigger than usual affair, and the then chief of police, Selim Zaki Pasha, personally went to handle the situation.

Many of the students by now had arms. Someone lobbed a grenade at the chief of police, and he was carried away a dying man. With the death of Selim Zaki Pasha, Premier Nokrashy decided it was high time he put down his foot firmly, before he lost all control of the situation.

Nokrashy Pasha felt that the Muslim Brotherhood was at the root of most of the trouble. The premier issued an ultimatum to the Brotherhood to return to their original raison d'être, of being a religious group wanting to propagate the teachings of the Koran. He warned them not to meddle in politics and leave that to those whose job it was to run the affairs of the country. The Brotherhood refused to listen to him and continued their political activities. They felt secure in their own strength and popular support.

I occasionally went to listen to Sheikh Hassan el Banna address the crowds at his headquarters not far from the famous Saladin's Citadel of Cairo. In those narrow streets where hundreds of thousands lived in squalor, Hassan el Banna found his most fervent members. Militant Islam appealed to them and seemed to offer them a chance for something better. The courtyard of the Brotherhood headquarters would be jammed with listeners and the streets outside packed with more thousands listening to the colorful speaker's voice coming through the loudspeakers. He appealed to their religious fervor, their nationalist spirit, their desire to better their situation, and also to the usually dormant aggressor instinct that seems to be in the soul of every man, until stirred into action by something or somebody.

Hassan el Banna definitely aroused the common people. It often caused them to commit acts that were ugly. But people who feel that they have been wronged and oppressed for centuries, who smart under real or imaginary injustices, do things that they normally would not do.

The fact remains, however, that the Muslim Brotherhood refused to go back to its original purpose of being a religious group. The leaders, some of whom were ambitious and aimed at getting the reins of government into their hands, felt that they had enough public support to defy the government.

Nokrashy Pasha had to take up this challenge. He therefore ordered the suppression of the Muslim Brotherhood party. He outlawed it, closed down their headquarters and their daily newspaper, seized their printing presses, and closed all their clubs throughout the country. Events moved quickly after that. Within a few days, the Muslim Brotherhood retaliated.

As Nokrashy Pasha entered the Ministry of Interior on the morning of December 28, 1948, a police officer approached, saluted him, and then drawing his revolver, pumped five bullets into his back. Nokrashy's bodyguard leaped in too late to protect their leader, but they caught his murderer. The police officer turned out to be a member of the Muslim Brotherhood who was not a police officer at all. He had bought the uniform, and conveniently disguised, entered the ministry. Policemen on duty thought he was a new officer assigned to the premier.

In a matter of hours, King Farouk had chosen Nokrashy's successor. Ibrahim Abdul Hadi Pasha, chief of the Royal Cabinet, became the new premier. Abdul Hadi Pasha, a relatively young man, had been Nokrashy Pasha's friend and deputy in the Saadist party. When the king wanted him to become chief of the Royal Cabinet, he resigned from the party as palace officials are supposed to be nonpartisan. Now he went back both as premier and leader of the Saadist party. He had been an active student youth leader in his younger days and knew the mentality of the crowds. Tall, tough, and considered one of the handsome men in Egyptian politics, Abdul Hadi Pasha started rounding up the Muslim Brotherhood immediately.

He countered terror by terror and struck savagely at the Brotherhood. Nokrashy Pasha's assassin was subjected to a tough third degree, and from the information obtained, more people connected with the murderer were arrested. In turn, they were questioned and from them the government started finding out about the party. Within a matter of days over two hundred members of the Brotherhood were arrested and arms caches unearthed. The government alleged that they had been gathering arms not to fight in Palestine, but to stage a coup d'état in Egypt and take over the government themselves.

Premier Ibrahim Abdul Hadi's tough tactics paralysed, at least for the time being, the activities of the Muslim Brotherhood. Rather than being on the offensive, they were forced back on the defensive. People who had jumped on the Muslim Brotherhood bandwagon quietly slipped away.

Shortly after, as Sheikh Hassan el Banna was stepping out of his car to visit some people, he was shot and killed. It was safely presumed that his killers were followers of Nokrashy Pasha, avenging the assassination of their own leader.

With the death of Sheikh el Banna, what little power the Muslim Brotherhood had managed to retain was quickly dissipated by disagreements among his principal lieutenants. The basic appeal of the organization, however, remained ever present, awaiting the arrival of a new leader to revive and direct the religious fervor of the average Egyptian into a well-organized body. It was some years before a new crisis appeared that paved the way for the resuscitation of the Muslim Brotherhood.

Ibrahim Abdul Hadi Pasha continued in power until July 1949. He maintained a tough policy of repression designed to stamp out communism, any possible Muslim Brotherhood activities, and too much criticism of the Palestine war. Censorship remained in vigor and was attacked by the press. People were generally dissatisfied.

Without much warning, King Farouk one day replaced Abdul Hadi Pasha with Hussein Sirry Pasha, a small, portly, independent nonparty man. Not a popular leader, Sirry Pasha was nevertheless respected as a blunt, cigar-smoking businessman. His job was to prepare the general elections in the country. Under a party cabinet, elections were almost sure to have been suspect by the opposition. So, the nonpartisan Sirry Pasha went ahead with his preparations. On January 8, 1950, the Wafdist party was returned to power by a strong majority. Mustapha el Nahas Pasha was once more in the saddle, and people wondered what the new government would produce.

Nahas Pasha mixed his cabinet, bringing in some of his old cronies and quite a few younger elements. He gave some of the key posts to young men. The Ministry of Foreign Affairs went to Mohamed Salah el Din, lawyer, businessman, and writer, who had often voiced his opinions about foreign affairs. The Ministry of Social Affairs was handed to Ahmed Hussein, a well-known and respected expert in this field. Nahas Pasha's second in command in the party, Fouad Serag el Dine Pasha, took over the Ministry of Interior.

The new Wafdist government started off with an ambitious program both in domestic and foreign affairs. Each of the new ministers was trying to prove his mettle, and, to do them justice, many of them had excellent projects. Ahmed Hussein, later made a Pasha, immediately started a series of social reforms and presented constructive bills to Parliament. Salah el Dine Bey, also later made a Pasha, said his aim was to achieve the national aspirations of Egypt.

As minister of education, Nahas Pasha had chosen Taha Hussein, prominent man of letters, idolized by the students. Taha Hussein, the blind man who wanted all other Egyptians to read, immediately announced that his aim was to make education free in primary and secondary schools and to build more universities.

There were certain disagreements in the cabinet, and some changes were made within a year or two. Youthful Zaki Abdel Mota'al Bey resigned from the Ministry of Finance, and Fuad Serag el Dine Pasha added this portfolio to his heavy duties as minister of interior and secretary-general of the Wafdist party. Not long after, Ahmed Hussein Pasha, considered by many as one of the most promising young leaders in Egypt, disagreed with some of his colleagues and resigned.

The cabinet was weakened by internal disagreements and the general dissatisfaction of masses. Few, if any, of the great projects had been achieved. Most had not even been started and still remained in their blueprint stage, or worse still, just a vague idea in the minds of the ministers. The cost of living was increasing, and the government seemed to be doing little to combat that trend. Many people accused the government of nepotism, corruption, and stagnation.

During that period, the gradual resurgence of the still outlawed Muslim Brotherhood was noticed by observers, as was the appearance of a new political group, the socialists. In the elections that had brought Nahas Pasha to power, one socialist made his debut in the Chamber of Deputies. It was the first time in the parliamentary history of Egypt that a socialist had appeared. He was Ibrahim Shukry, deputy leader of the party. His boss, Ahmed Hussein (not to be confused with his namesake, the minister of social affairs), had failed in the elections, but things were looking up for the leftists.

Ahmed Hussein started a weekly paper, *Al Ishtirakia* (*Socialism*), whose sales rocketed amazingly. He attacked the government, capitalists, the British, foreign firms, and a host of others. He demanded reforms. His articles often seemed to follow the Communist party line. His appeal can be gauged by the results of his campaign against Pepsi-Cola and Coca-Cola. He charged that Pepsi-Cola contained pepsin, which came from pigs—forbidden to all Muslims by their religion. Pepsi-Cola was colored by drops of pig's blood, and Coca-Cola contained harmful drugs. He appealed to the Egyptians to boycott these drinks of the American capitalists who, backed by Egyptian millionaires, were "harming the people." The tremendous sales of those two organizations dropped to almost zero throughout the country. In many places salesmen were assaulted. By appealing to both the religious and social feelings of the masses, Ahmed Hussein struck very effectively.

It is said that he had conducted the campaigns against them because the two companies had refused to buy any advertising space in his newspaper. Whether that is true or not, it became evident that his paper could have considerable influence over the people.

Faced with mounting criticism of domestic affairs, and having done little to fulfill the national aspirations of the country, Nahas Pasha's cabinet found itself in a shaky position. Conversations had dragged on with the British over both the Sudan and the evacuation of British troops from the Suez Canal zone. Salah el Din had gone to London to talk the matter over with the then foreign secretary, Ernest Bevin. Other talks had been conducted in Egypt between the Egyptian government and the British ambassador, Sir Ralph Stevenson. Field Marshal Sir William Slim, chief of the imperial general staff, had also conferred with Egyptian political and military leaders.

There had been no meeting of the minds, no apparent solution that the two sides would accept. For fifteen months, the two sides had haggled in a series of meetings, presenting aide-mémoire after aide-mémoire and coming back to the same arguments they had mulled for weeks and months.

XIII
Abrogation of Anglo-Egyptian Agreements

The talks had been endless and were not progressing. In point of fact, their tone was becoming worse. Salah el Din Pasha warned that unless some speedy answer to his proposals was forthcoming, he would submit a full report to the Egyptian Parliament on the talks, which he would break off. Sir Ralph Stevenson warned that breaking off the talks and making public statements from which it would be difficult to retreat could affect the relations of the two countries.

Discussing the question of the British troops on the Suez Canal, the British ambassador pointed out a "common approach to the problem of defence" must be worked out. Unless proper defence plans were laid down, Egypt might be faced with two invasions, he said—one from the Russians to occupy the country and the other from the West when the Western powers would return to expel the aggressor.

"By a common scheme of defence you certainly have a good chance of escaping invasion just as happened in the last two wars. I am sure it is not impossible to find some common approach to the question of defence," said Sir Ralph.

In his reply Salah el Din Pasha pointed out among other things that the continued presence of British troops in Egypt was contrary to the United Nations resolution providing for the necessity of evacuating foreign troops from the territories of states occupied without their consent. The Egyptian foreign minister added that while he realized the United Nations Charter provided for regional agreements, these agreements were to be reached by mutual consent and not by force. Egypt felt her own army could defend the Suez Canal in peacetime, and in the event of any aggression the United Nations, and not Britain alone, should dispatch a force to repel invaders.

In September, when matters were reaching a deadlock between Britain and Egypt, the other Western powers and Turkey started taking a greater interest in the problem. They had been studying a proposed Middle East pact for some time, but now accelerated their blueprint to submit it to Egypt before relations worsened.

But the high state of tension through the country prompted Premier Nahas Pasha to stand up in Parliament on October 8, 1951, and declare: "In the interests of Egypt, I signed the 1936 treaty and in the interests of Egypt today, I ask you to abrogate it." In this speech, the ageing Egyptian premier definitely closed the door to any further talks with Britain and unilaterally abrogated the 1936 treaty and the 1899 condominium agreements concerning the Sudan.

There was wild enthusiasm both among the masses and in the Parliament. Everybody had been expecting the prime minister to announce the closing of Parliament for a delayed summer recess and to declare that the Anglo-Egyptian deadlock would be tackled again when Parliament reconvened. Demonstrations promptly followed the announcement. Students and workers paraded through the streets, shouting anti-British slogans. As could be expected some of the extremist elements indulged in some stone throwing, breaking up Coca-Cola trucks, shop windows belonging to foreign firms, and even indiscriminately breaking up Egyptian-owned offices.

The police stepped in and controlled the situation. In the meantime the various political parties gathered to plan their future course of action. The Wafdists were the heroes of the day, but everybody now wanted to pitch in.

The British government quickly came out with a statement that it would not recognize the abrogation of the treaties. Egypt's Parliament met again, passed the bills, and sent them to King Farouk for signature. When the decrees were signed, they became law. The treaty was no longer in force, as far as the Egyptians were concerned, and King Farouk had become king of Egypt and the Sudan.

The United States government, France, and other nations quickly rejected Egypt's action and refused to recognize any unilateral abrogation of an agreement. At the same time, the United States, Britain, France, and Turkey submitted a proposal to Egypt for a Middle East defence pact that would replace the Anglo-Egyptian treaty. Britain made new proposals for the Sudan that would include the supervision of the United States. Here are the texts of the proposals submitted to Egypt:

> Jefferson Caffery, the American Ambassador, Sir Ralph S. Stevenson, the British Ambassador, Maurice Couve de Murville, the French Ambassador and Hulusi A. Foat Tugay, the Turkish Ambassador, presented on Saturday, the following proposals to the Egyptian Foreign Minister H. E. Salah el Din Pasha:
>
> 1. Egypt belongs to the free world and in consequence her defence and that of the Middle East in general is equally vital to the other democratic nations.
>
> 2. The defence of Egypt and of the other countries in the Middle East against aggression from without can only be secured by the co-operation of all the interested powers.
>
> 3. The defence of Egypt can only be assured through the effective defence of the Middle East area and the coordination of this defence with that of adjacent areas.
>
> 4. It, therefore, seems desirable to establish an Allied Middle East Command in which countries able and willing to contribute to the defence of the area should participate. The United

Kingdom, the United States, France and Turkey are prepared to participate with the other interested countries in establishing such a command, Australia, New-Zealand and the Union of South Africa have moreover indicated their interest in the defence of the area and have agreed in principle to participate in the Command.

5. Egypt is invited to participate as a founder member of the Allied Middle East Command on a basis of equality and partnership with the other founder members.

6. If Egypt is prepared to cooperate fully in the Allied Middle East Command Organization, in accordance with the provisions of the attached Annex, His Majesty's Government for their part would be willing to agree to the suppression of the 1936 treaty and would also be willing to agree to withdraw from Egypt such British forces as are not allocated to the Allied Middle East Command by agreement between the Egyptian Government and the governments of the other countries also participating as founder members in the Allied Middle East Organization.

7. As regards the armed forces to be placed at the disposal of the Allied Middle East Command and the provision to that Command of the necessary strategic defence facilities such as military and air bases, communications, ports, etc., Egypt will be expected to make her contribution on the same footing as the other participating powers.

8. In keeping with the spirit of these arrangements, Egypt would be invited to accept a position of high authority and responsibility within the Allied Middle East Command and to designate Egyptian officers for integration in the Allied Middle East Command headquarters staff.

9. Facilities to train and equip her forces will be given to Egypt by those participating members of the Allied Command.

10. The detailed organisation of the Allied Middle East Defence Organisation and its exact relationship with the North Atlantic Treaty Organisation have yet to be worked out in consultation between all the powers concerned. For this purpose, it is proposed that all founding members of the Allied Middle East Command should send military representatives to a meeting to be held in the

near future with the object of preparing detailed proposals for submission to the government concerned.

Annex

1. In common with the other participating powers who are making similar contributions to the defence of the area:

a) Egypt will agree to furnish to the proposed Allied Middle East Command Organisation such strategic defence and other facilities on her soil as are indispensable for the organisation in peacetime of the defence of the Middle East.

b) She will undertake to grant the forces of the Allied Middle East Command all the necessary facilities and assistance in the event of war, the imminent menace of war, or apprehended international emergency—including the use of Egyptian ports, airfields and means of communication.

2. It would also be hoped that Egypt would agree to the Allied Supreme Commander's Headquarters being located in her territory.

3. In keeping with the spirit of these arrangements, it would be understood:

a) That the present British Base in Egypt would be formally handed over to Egypt on the understanding that it would simultaneously become an Allied Base within the Allied Middle East Command with full Egyptian participation in the running of this base in peace and war.

b) That the strength of the Allied forces of the participating nations to be stations in Egypt in peace time would be determined between the participating nations, including Egypt, from time to time as progress is made in building up the forces of the Allied Middle East Command.

4. It would also be understood that an air defence organisation, including both Egyptian and Allied forces, would be set up under the command of an officer with joint responsibility to the Egyptian Government and to the Allied Middle East Command for the protection of Egypt and the Allied base.

* * *

The four-power proposals were immediately rejected by the Egyptian government, which gave no reason for refusing them. It maintained the attitude that nothing would be discussed before the evacuation of British troops and the recognition of Egypt and the Sudan as an united, indivisible nation under the Egyptian crown.

Among the people, the hitherto quiet Muslim Brotherhood again appeared as a powerful, popular group. A new leader had been appointed, Hassan el Hudeiby Bey, former judge. The various parties and youth organisations started forming ''liberation battalions'' to wage an underground war on the British. Pamphlets and posters appeared urging the crowd to boycott British goods and appealing to the laborers in British camps to abandon their jobs. The government promised them all work if they did not cooperate with the British.

On October 16, demonstrations took place throughout the country to celebrate the final abrogation of the treaty and the decree making King Farouk ruler of Egypt and the Sudan. The first shots were fired in Ismailia, one of the three towns on the Suez Canal. Angry demonstrators, seeing British trucks going through the town, threw stones at them and attacked a British army grocery store where wives and children of soldiers were shopping. The hate-filled, furious demonstrators set fire to some trucks and tried to set fire to the grocery. Suddenly a battalion of the Sixth Lancashire Fusilliers, supported by armored cars, arrived on the scene and opened fire on the demonstrators. Eight Egyptians were killed, and seventy-four wounded.

Other demonstrations occurred that same day at Port Said when demonstrators attacked British army trucks and burned eleven. Troops appeared and fired at the crowds, killing five and wounding about thirty.

The British had obviously been prepared for quick action in the event of any Egyptians staging attacks on British families or troops. British tanks rumbled into Ismailia, occupied the town, cordonned off the native quarters, and erected checkposts, barbed wire, and posted their men at all strategic points. Quickly they took over control of all customs, roads, railways, and telephone communications from the Egyptian authorities. All bridges linking Egypt with Sinai were occupied by the British.

This isolated the better part of the Egyptian army stationed in Gaza and along the Palestine border. When the British captured El Ferdan bridge, the only railbridge over the Suez Canal, they had to attack a small Egyptian army force there, killing two men and wounding five. So rapidly and forcefully did the British move that the Egyptians were left paralysed. The British continued to act very tough, but after the first speechless reaction of the Egyptians, the pent-up emotions of the people burst again in a series of violent demonstrations which the police found difficult to handle.

"Give us arms," shouted the mobs, cursing Britain, painting over all signs that were not written in Arabic, and breaking up various shops despite efforts from the police. Amazingly, no foreigners were killed in the subsequent days. The police dispersed the mobs, using tear gas and sometimes firing buckshot into them. Demonstrations were quickly forbidden and the government made it clear that any further demonstrations would be dealt with severely. Sarag el Din Pasha explained that Egypt's dispute was neither with the foreigners living in Egyptian cities nor even with British civilians, but with the British government and the troops in the Canal zone.

Calm was restored in the Egyptian cities, but it was a tense situation on the Canal zone. Egyptian native labor, on whom the British troops depended, started walking out of the camps. Within a few days, the labor shortage became serious. Organised units of Egyptians started preventing any Egyptians who wanted to work with the British from reaching their destinations, turning them back on the road and threatening them. British troops got tough, threw out of the Canal zone Egyptian officers they thought were inciting the people to adopt this policy of noncooperation with the British. They caught the head of the seamen's union and threw him out of the zone. They searched all traffic going in and out of the Suez Canal zone to see that no arms were smuggled through.

British reinforcements were rushed into the area from Cyprus and from England. The Royal Navy sent several ships there to guard the waters. British families of troops were evacuated from the cities, and many sent home, while others were grouped into well-protected zones inside the Canal area.

The British general elections saw the return of Winston Churchill and his Tory government. Anthony Eden, the man who had helped create the Arab League, replaced Herbert Morrison as foreign secretary, and once again handled Egyptian problems. It was Eden who had headed the British delegation in 1936 that signed a treaty with Egypt.

The tough tactics of the British caused a mounting hatred against them throughout Egypt. Many moderate Egyptians thought that the British were being unnecessarily provocative, regardless of the actions of the Egyptian government. Every day there were incidents in which the British Tommies manhandled Egyptians. Poorly equipped and obviously unable to openly oppose the British, the Egyptians resorted to passive resistance. Many extremist elements wanted to go further, but the government restrained them. It would have been suicidal to attack the British, yet many thought that death might be better than just passive resistance.

Those in favor of some kind of a treaty with Russia gained strength in the country. Several sought a nonaggression pact with Russia. Demonstrators, before the ban against public gatherings, had gathered in thousands in front of the Russian legation cheering the Soviets wildly and demanding arms and a treaty. It was the first time such a demonstration had taken place and many were justifiably alarmed by this.

Many felt that the United States had better step in with some concrete proposals before the Egyptians turned over completely to the Russians. Already the masses were feeling very much that way. Too much delay might upset the existing government. The Suez Canal area would not serve as a useful base without the cooperation of the Egyptians, and in the event of a Russian invasion, there would be the constant danger of a huge fifth column against the Western forces.

No one saw the solution, but many hoped that the Americans would produce something acceptable to all.

XIV
Palestine Divided

The Holy Land of Palestine, sacred to Christians, Muslims, and Jews alike, has been the target of many an invader through the centuries. It was still a disputed area after two world wars that by force or negotiation had settled many a problem. But even two world wars brought no solution to that small, barren wasteland that so many seemed to covet for different reasons and purposes.

The beginnings of Zionism are well known to all students of Middle Eastern history, and the rise of the Arab nationalist movements is equally a matter of record. Suffice it to say that Arabs and Jews held conflicting views concerning the ultimate destiny of Palestine. With the end of World War I, Britain sought and obtained mandatory powers over Palestine, which General Allenby had conquered in 1917 with the help of an Arab army formed by the now legendary Lawrence of Arabia and the sons of Sherif Hussein.

The Palestine war started then and has since continued with an occasional break. It is from those days that various figures who even now hold the stage made their entry, and it is those early years which moulded them into their present form.

There were many promises made by the British during the First World War, and as far as Palestine was concerned, these promises were flagrantly contradictory. The Arabs thought they would have an Arab kingdom that would include Palestine. The

Jews obtained the Balfour Declaration promising them a national home. Later, various secret agreements were revealed that showed even more conflicting agreements.

In those early days of the Arab revolt against the Turks, a young officer in the Turkish army, an Arab educated in Constantinople, abandoned his former overlords to join the army that would fight the Turks and be rewarded by the creation of an independent Arab kingdom. He fought well, and when the Turks had been beaten, he started recruiting an army for the man who was destined to rule the new Arab kingdom, King Feisal. The young officer worked enthusiastically for the realisation of his youthful dreams—the birth of a new, proud, free Arab kingdom.

He travelled the length and breadth of the Arab lands, from Syria to Iraq, Lebanon, Palestine, and Jordan, rallying the young men to the banner of King Feisal, the first ruler of a united Arab nation. But the secret agreements of the great powers, the decision carving those lands into mandates under foreign supervision, and the expulsion of Feisal from his Arab capital of Damascus, shattered the dreams of the young idealist.

Feisal was given a consolation prize—the kingdom of Iraq, with Baghdad as capital and the British to hold mandatory powers until such time as Feisal could rule alone. Syria, with Damascus, was given to the French. The British took over Palestine and Jerusalem, the birthplace of this young Arab officer. Not only did they take it over, but they started allowing Zionists to enter the Holy Land.

Disillusioned and consumed by a burning hatred against the British, the young Arab officer who had fought alongside Lawrence turned against the English with all the tremendous energy at his command. It was the beginning of a long road strewn with imprisonment, exile, and intrigue. It was a road that took him to many places, and guided his actions for decades to come.

That young man was Amin el Husseini, later to become grand mufti of Jerusalem, and president of the Palestine Arab party. It was the aftermath of World War I that charted the subsequent life of the most notorious of all Palestinians, Haj Amin, or as his followers often called him, "Mufti Effendi."

The course of other men who played their important roles in the destiny of Palestine were also affected by this same early period. One of the four leaders of the Arab revolt was Emir Abdullah, son of Sherif Hussein of Mecca and brother of Feisal, who had been destined to rule the Arab kingdom of Syria. Abdullah's consolation prize was the desolate Emirate of Transjordan, a barren land east of the river Jordan. Abdullah had been moving up from Mecca with an army to help Feisal against the French in Syria. The then colonial secretary of the British government, Winston Churchill, stopped him. Subsequently, Abdullah was made emir of the area where he halted. Thus was Transjordan born, an emirate under British mandate.

While Haj Amin developed an all-consuming hatred for the British, King Abdullah accepted matters as they developed and with time became Britain's greatest ally in the Arab world. Even when the British let him down, as they did on occasion, this patient, wily ruler understood that it was not to spite him and swallowed his disappointment. To the day of his assassination, he firmly believed that his policy of befriending the British would prove, in the long run, the wisest policy for the Arab world in general and himself in particular.

And, to give him his due credit, once he had made up his mind about his long-range policy, he stuck to it. Even in the darkest hours of Britain's history, during the early part of World War II, he was loyal to his friends. When every other ally had been defeated, and with the United States not yet in the war, Abdullah's Arab Legion fought alongside the British in the Middle East against tremendous odds.

Rightly or wrongly, and only history will be able to judge, King Abdullah had chosen his allies and stuck to them through thick and thin.

Another man of the ''Arab revolt'' clique is Nuri es Said Pasha, the perennial prime minister of Iraq. He led a force of Egyptians and fought alongside Lawrence and General Allenby. When Feisal was driven out of his capital of Damascus by the French, Nuri Pasha was one of the Iraq leaders who invited him to become the king of Iraq. Ever since, Nuri Pasha loyally served the descendants of King Feisal and followed a very pro-British line that has won the criticism of several Iraq and Arab nationalists. His pro-British leanings twice drove him out of Iraq when military coups d'états were directed successfully against him. But he always returned and maintained his policy, until his death in 1958 when mobs in Baghdad killed him and his king, the young King Faisal II.

Haj Amin, King Abdullah, and Nuri Pasha were to have important roles in the Palestine story.

Between World War I and World War II, the Arabs continually opposed the British policy of allowing Zionists into Palestine. At times, the Arabs revolted and savage fighting took place in the hills and plains between the British and the Palestine Arabs.

In 1929 the British had to put down a serious revolt using considerable armed forces. Then in 1936, the Palestine Arabs, aided by volunteer groups from neighbouring Arab states, rose again. Peasants and tribesmen formed guerilla gangs and the politicians took to the hills from where, to the best of their limited military ability, they directed the operations. It was at that time that a youthful Arab became one of the more notorious of the guerilla leaders. He was Faouzi el Kaoukji, a tough, bullet-headed, red-haired, blue-eyed Lebanese from Tripoli.

The British were very hard with the Palestine Arabs. There were mass arrests of civilians and villagers and collective fines, while the RAF bombed population centers. Emergency defence regulations gave almost unlimited liberty to the military authorities to execute saboteurs and those suspected of sabotage on the slightest pretext.

When World War II broke out, the Arabs were still continuing their resistance despite the British attacks and the arrest and exile of many of their leaders. The revolt was called off "for the duration."

During the war the country was filled with American, British, and Allied forces. Air bases dotted the countryside, and Palestine remained a busy military zone until the war started receding from the Middle East and the Balkans.

The war had not yet finished when the first Zionist blows against the British took place. The horrors of Nazi Germany had determined the Jews to establish their national homeland in Palestine, and the movement to the promised land had started. Illegal immigration was organised despite the efforts of the British to prevent it. Once in a while, they would intercept a broken-down boat jammed with Jewish immigrants, and they would be shipped to Cyprus where big camps were organized for them.

In Palestine itself, various Zionist extremists organized their own terrorist bands to strike at the British. They wanted to build their state of Israel and resented the restrictions the British were trying to impose. The story of the Jewish struggle against the British mandatory authorities is a long, bitter one. It is a story of political move and countermove, and of terrorist activities carried out by desperate men and women, with much imagination and brilliant execution.

They were often ruthless, but they claimed they had no alternative. The Jewish terrorists killed, dynamited buildings, kidnapped and whipped British officers and men, staged commando attacks on police fortresses, and turned all of Palestine into a maze of barbed wire. They gave the British no respite.

In the United States, clever Jewish lobbyists won the support of the press and radio, and world opinion was very much against the British whose thankless task it was to maintain a semblance of law and order in the Holy Land. At the same time, the Arab League was also starting to turn against British policy in Palestine. The Arabs blasted the Jews and cursed the British. Both Arabs and Jews were building up forces for the final showdown. The British decided that the whole problem was not worth the expense and announced their decision to pull out of Palestine by May 15, 1948.

Neither Jews nor Arabs really believed them, but both started laying down some organisation to replace the British. The Jews already had the Jewish agency that for years had existed as a shadow cabinet. The Arabs had nothing much outside the Palestine Arab Higher Committee headed by the exiled Haj Amin. They issued communiqués but did little to establish a constructive form of government which would ultimately replace the British.

After a while it began to look as if the British were really going to get out. They started organizing their evacuation. It was then that the Arabs and the Jews began considering the immediate future seriously and seeing that sooner or later they would have to fight it out.

On the Jewish side, the groundwork had already been laid. The terrorist organisations and the secret underground Zionist army, the Haganah, with its efficient commando force, the Palmach, were well capable of forming the nucleus of a solid Jewish army. The Arabs, on the other hand, had some veterans of the old 1936 revolt, both in and out of Palestine, but they had to start from scratch, building up their guerrilla bands.

Such leaders as Haj Amin el Husseini and Faouzi el Kaoukji were back from their lengthy stay in Axis-occupied Europe during the war. Haj Amin had sought and obtained refuge in Egypt. Faouzi el Kaoukji suddenly reached Cairo from Europe, and there was great speculation about the role he would play in any subsequent fighting in Palestine. He was staying at the Continental Hotel and receiving a continual flow of visitors, mainly older people he had known in the past revolts and some younger people wanting to join him in his fight against the Jews.

Like Haj Amin, Kaoukji had decided that only the Axis might help the Arabs get rid of the British, and of course, of the Jews. So, again like Haj Amin, he had participated in the Rashid Aly pro-Axis revolt in Iraq. He was seriously wounded when a Royal Air Force plane strafed him, but managed to be carried out of the Middle East and into Europe.

My first meeting with him was at the Continental Hotel in Cairo. He placed himself at the "disposal of the Arab people, should they ask me to fight or lead the people in the fight. I will do so against anybody who opposes the freedom of the Arabs." He had grown a bit older and stouter, but he still held himself stiff as a ramrod, despite his wounds. Like many other leaders, he had been trained in the Ottoman army. He had a thick neck, red hair that was thinning, small blue eyes, thick lips, and widely spaced teeth. His close-cropped hair added the finishing touch to a man who might have easily passed for a Prussian general.

From the beginning he blasted the British and sounded the call for arms to save Palestine. "The British should know better than to give in to the Zionists, thereby endangering their whole relations with the Arab world. The West is seeking to secure itself against any possible danger from the East, and one sure way for Britain would be to strengthen her friendship with the Arabs rather than to antagonize them.

"So far the Arabs have been willing to be patient, to negotiate and use diplomatic and peaceful methods to convince the British that their interests lie in befriending us and not submitting to pressure from Zionism. If peaceful methods fail, then the British who negotiated will find that the same Arabs who negotiated are also able to fight, and, as they have fought in the past, will fight with all the means at their disposal. We will die fighting rather than accept to give away our land." Shortly after, El Kaoukji left for Beirut and Damascus where he met other friends and started working on building a new Arab guerilla army to fight.

By the beginning of 1948, it was becoming evident that the Arabs and Jews would soon clash, and that the conflict would increase in intensity as the two sides stepped up their preparations. The Arab League had held several meetings, mainly in secret, and had hinted of war plans. Guerilla groups were formed inside Palestine under the command of such young people as Abdel Kader el Husseini, a cousin of the grand mufti. Local leaders were appearing in various Arab districts, and in the beginning there was little coordination between them all.

Outside Palestine, Faouzi el Kaoukji was building a volunteer guerilla army of non-Palestinian Arabs, who would go into the Holy Land with him to aid their Palestinian brothers. For the moment, and on the surface at least, the rivalries between various Arab groups had been buried. It was hinted that if the British left on May 15, Arab forces of the regular armies would enter Palestine from all sides.

By the beginning of February, I had moved over from Egypt to the Levant. Beirut had become my temporary base, and I travelled between Lebanon, Syria, Transjordan, and Palestine itself. At the time I met such leaders as Iraqi Gen. Ismail Safwat Pasha, supreme commander of all Arab volunteer forces; Kaoukji again; Gen. Taha el Hashimi, the Iraqi who had been appointed inspector general of all Arab guerilla forces; Abdel Kader el Husseini, who commanded the Palestine Arab forces in the Jerusalem area; and other lesser leaders.

They all told me the same story. The Arab forces were now ready to enter Palestine and start large-scale operations against the Zionist forces. They claimed they were well-equipped and said they had enough supplies and arms in reserve to ensure their continued maintenance for a long period.

Plans had been completed to coordinate the operations of the Palestinian Arab fighters and the "forces of liberation" expected to enter the Holy Land from the different neighbouring states. The Palestine Arab fighters, who had previously received their orders from the Palestine Arab Higher Commitee of Haj Amin, were now placed under the command of the Arab Military Committee created by the Arab League and whose headquarters were in Damascus.

Through Egypt and Lebanon, arms were reported to be transiting into Palestine where the British, still technically running the country, were too busy with their evacuation plans to maintain their previous vigilance on the frontiers. Many Iraqis, Syrians, and Lebanese had crossed into Palestine already and were lying low waiting for the orders to start operations. Some small raids against isolated Jewish settlements had taken place but without success, although they were tremendously boosted in the local Arab press.

Generally, the Arab plan—such as it was—was divided into two sections. The first phase was to include all operations undertaken while the British were still in Palestine, and the second, expected to be far more widespread, after the British evacuation of the Holy Land. El Kaoukji was expected to enter Palestine to take over the command of all Arab guerillas in the Northern Palestine area, leaving southern Palestine to the Egyptians. Arab forces would start a series of raids against the Zionists, especially in outlying settlements, communications, and, ultimately, against Jewish-held towns.

The second phase of the operations would come after the British evacuated, and the way was clear for the Arab regular armies to participate in gaining control of the country in the name of the Palestine Arab population.

Around the end of January 1948, I wrote in my notes, after several meetings with various Arab leaders:

> Arab troops now completely surround Palestine, while within the Holy Land, armed Arab forces have already taken up positions

according to an overall plan which will be carried out in different phases.

The Army of Liberation's first four thousand men are already in Palestine working with the locally recruited and trained Arabs, while several thousands—it is impossible to give an estimate—are waiting for Gen. Ismail Safwat's orders to cross the border, with Faouzi el Kaoukji at their head.

All around Palestine, troops of the various Arab regular armies are posted, forming a ring around the war-torn Holy Land. To the south, considerable Egyptian forces including the best artillery units are concentrated at el Arish and Rafa, by the coast. In the hinterland, Egyptians have small detachments at various points of the Egypto-Palestinian frontier.

King Abdullah's mechanized Arab Legion is both within and outside Palestine. Some units are serving with the British inside Palestine, while others are maintaining a vigilant watch over the Jordan.

Syrian and Lebanese regulars dot the Palestine border. Jeep-borne patrols scurry back and forth along the frontiers and occasionally carry out manoeuvres within sight of the Zionist settlements on the other side.

While the regular armies have ringed Palestine, the Arab High Command in Damascus has given its final orders for the definite line-up within the Holy Land.

The entire North Palestine area has been entrusted to Faouzi el Kaoukji, in whose area lie most of the Jewish settlements of Palestine. Both the cities of Haifa and Tel Aviv are within Kaoukji's field of operations. He will command his own army and all local Palestinian Arab fighters in that area.

Operations in and around the city of Jaffa, just outside Tel Aviv, are in the hands of a Syrian who up until recently was a senior officer in the regular army (I never got his name). He will defend Jaffa and strike from there at nearby Jewish settlements to clear the Jaffa-Lydda-Jerusalem road from all threats. Occasionally, he will coordinate his operations with attacks which Faouzi el Kaoukji may want to make on Tel-Aviv, the Zionist stronghold in Palestine.

The operations in and around Jerusalem are conducted by Abdel Kader el Husseini, whose forces will be reinforced by trained volunteers from other Arab countries. Abdel Kader has already received sizeable quantities of arms and more are reported to be flowing to him.

Lydda area has been assigned to Sheikh Hassan Salameh, German-trained commando and paratrooper, who will also be supported by units from the Arab Liberation army. The Egyptian commander whose name is not yet divulged, will lead them. They are reported to be ready to cross whenever General Safwat gives the signal.

By that time, Damascus had become the military capital of the Arab world. The old storied capital with its famous souks and its biblical street called Straight had once more taken the martial aspect it had when Saladin set forth to fight the crusaders in Palestine. The city teemed with soldiers in different uniforms—U.S. uniforms worn by the Syrian regular army, the befezzed volunteers, Druzes and Bedouins wearing the desert headdress, jeep-borne units, truckloads of soldiers, and crash-helmeted dispatch riders roaring down the modern avenues on their motorcycles.

In a modest house on one of the main streets of new Damascus, lived Kaoukji, directing operations in North Palestine. Already his forces had carried out a few minor skirmishes with the Jews.

I went to see him at his house. There had been talks that he would soon go to Palestine himself, and I wanted to make sure that I would be among those who would accompany him. At the same time, I wanted to get an interview from him, and he, as usual, started by refusing to talk, then ended up by talking a great deal.

He started by saying that Arab actions so far in Palestine were "nothing to what will soon come." Kaoukji attacked the policy of the United States and said that all chances of American interests prospering in the Middle East had vanished.

"We have not really started, but soon the world will see what stuff Arab fighters are made of," he added. From the very beginning Kaoukji had underestimated the strength of the Jewish forces. On this occasion he told me, "The Jews have fooled the Americans and others by stating they will be able to defend themselves against the Arabs, not only the Palestinians, but all the Arab armies. Now—before we have really started our fight—they are wailing and pleading for an international army and assistance. We are mounting a campaign that will destroy the so-called Zionist army and state." He also said that he was working around the clock both at home and at his headquarters. He often went to see the training of volunteers at Kattana camp near Damascus but refused to allow me or any other correspondent to see the camp and its trainees.

Kaoujki's home was a colorful affair. All around it were his human watchdogs, who day and night roamed around and never allowed anyone to approach the house without one of them acting as escort. Most of the sentries wore GI uniforms and sported the Bedouin headdress. In one of the large rooms a variety of Arabs kept flowing in to pay homage to Kaoukji and enlist in his "Liberation army." In an inner chamber sat the quiet, handsome Capt. Mahmoud Rifai, graduate of Potsdam Military Academy and now acting as Kaoukji's aide. He had "resigned" from the Syrian army to work with the guerilla leader.

More than any other Arab country, Syria had become Palestine-conscious and worked for the Palestine cause. Whether out of hopes of emerging as the unchallenged leaders of the Arab world or because of the sincere conviction of the people, the government was going all out, and the people responded. The Ministry of National Defence, headed by swarthy, youthful Ahmed Sharabaty, had turned over its offices to the Arab High

Command and worked closely with them. Shops displayed posters asking the people to contribute to the Palestine cause.

"Volunteer or contribute" had become the slogan. The government issued a Palestine tax on practically everything. Volunteers were given a free run of Damascus when on leave, although they had their own special military police to survey them.

In the first days of February, Haj Amin el Husseini reached Damascus from Cairo. This was the signal for more secret huddles between various Arab politicians and the military leaders. Already men of the Liberation Army were in Palestine. In the Jerusalem area, the Palestine Arabs led by Abdel Kader el Husseini were almost daily clashing with the Zionists, and sometimes with the British. The Arabs held Kastel and Bab el Wad, controlling the road from the coast to Jerusalem.

With the arrival of the notorious Haj Amin, observers realized that within a short time there would be some dramatic developments. It became an open secret that shortly Kaoukji would enter Palestine to take over the operations there, once the talks with the mufti had ended. Soon after the mufti's arrival, Abdel Kader Husseini and Sheikh Salameh, who had both been inside Palestine with their forces, reached Damascus to talk matters over with the other Arab leaders. Thus, virtually every Arab leader who was going to take an active part in the Palestine campaign was in the Syrian capital.

We heard many reports about their decisions—that they had established the necessary liaison between the various sectors, and the appointment of the military commanders and their responsibilities confirmed. So far, they said, the various actions in Palestine were individual acts and uncoordinated, but now the organized, planned campaign was going to start.

I tried to get Kaoukji to allow me to go into Palestine with his forces, but he refused to grant me permission. He just half promised to take me along when he went, but even that was not sure. In any case, I learned that he was not planning to go in at the moment.

I decided to return to Beirut for a few days to see what was going on there and find out whether it would not be easier to accompany those volunteers who were entering Palestine from the Lebanese frontiers, without my having to wait for permission from Kaoukji. After all, while he was the most colorful of the leaders, he was not the top man, and I thought that perhaps some of Haj Amin's friends in Beirut would help me.

A young Lebanese newspaperman, Rashad Barbir (senior reporter at *Al Hayat*—a leading Beirut daily newspaper), told me he was willing to make a try to get across into Palestine. "If we can find one of the meeting places of the guerillas on the Lebanese side of the frontier, I know I shall have enough friends who will vouch for us and take us over," he told me.

So off we started in my little Citroen, down the coastal road from Beirut towards Tyre and Sidon. We stopped there and contacted some local notables whom Barbir knew, who vaguely told us that there had been quite a lot of traffic through some of the mountain roads towards Marjeyoun. There had been a lot of rain that year and the roads were very muddy. It was quite a trip. From Marjeyoun we kept on going towards the Palestine frontier, which was not very far away. We noticed that there was a good deal of traffic on the roads, and we just kept on going in the general direction of the border.

At one of the small mountain villages that overlooked the plains of Palestine, we ran into a horde of armed Arabs. As my car swung into the market place, we were quickly surrounded, and one man, looking and acting very tough, acted as spokesman. He wanted to see our identity cards. I introduced myself and Barbir.

The spokesman looked at me and then turned his attention to Barbir. Now Barbir is an honest to goodness Muslim Arab, who during the world war went to Germany to join Haj Amin's

Arab movement, such was his faith in the mufti and the Arab movement. But Barbir looks less like an Arab than anyone I know. He has flaming red hair and light blue eyes. His freckled face is very red and very un-Arab. It was not so much the presence of a correspondent that aroused their suspicion as Barbir. They thought he was a Jewish spy who spoke very good Arabic. Our identity cards were thoroughly examined, and we were grilled. I must confess that I passed several uncomfortable moments and prayed that the trigger-happy, hostile crowd would not become ugly.

Barbir then asked after several people he thought might be in the area. As he mentioned names, the curt answer was "He isn't here" or "never heard of him," but finally he hit on one name whose owner apparently was in the region. I was never happier to meet a man. He came up, opened his arms, and embraced Barbir. We were all set from then on. We were honored guests and allies. Anything we wanted to know would be told to us.

A guide took me to see a truck unloading rifles that were handed to the "Mojahideen"—fighters of the Jihad. They would come unarmed to this rendezvous, get their arms and ammunitions, and then slip over into Palestine. "You have come upon one of our concentrations. From here we cross into Palestine, which is just over the hilltop, and disperse to previously assigned positions," explained my guide. "This village is our storehouse for food. These trucks you see have brought rifles and ammunition which will be distributed to both our volunteers and to Palestinian Arabs across the border. We are well equipped and itching to get started."

The volunteers were in khaki uniforms with the Bedouin *hatta* and *egal* on their heads. The Palestine Arabs were not in uniform but dressed in their peasant costumes. All carried rifles and bandoliers slung across their shoulders. I walked up the hill and looked down on Palestine. My guide told me, "Over there are the Zionist settlements, while at differents spots of the frontier the British have increased their units. They have parachute regiment units, soldiers in armored cars, and Bren gun carriers. But the frontier is big and there are always places we can slip through, even in large numbers."

There had been several small skirmishes in which the Jews and Arabs had lost a few men, but nothing of major importance.

I drove all along the frontier area and saw other concentrations of Arabs. At one spot we watched a British armored car patrol start off from the town of Metulla on the Palestine side of the border. The patrol was one of many trying to watch the frontier and prevent any Arabs crossing over. As they set off through the winding mountain roads, Arab scouts watched their course, passed back the word, and those Arabs waiting to cross into the Holy Land merely walked in the other direction to that taken by the British and casually entered Palestine.

Meanwhile in London, Washington, and Lake Success, negotiations and talks were going on in an effort to find a peaceful solution to the problem. Partition had been rejected, and now the powers were trying to find a new formula. But at the same time, preparations were proceeding for war.

Little did the Arabs know then how futile their preparations were and how badly organized were their leaders. Even today, only incomplete versions have been revealed of their so-called secret huddles and of their allegedly coordinated plans. As they shook hands with each other and swore to put aside all differences in these difficult moments, each was sure that the other would double-cross him, and so each made his own plans to double-cross the other first.

The Arab leaders fooled themselves, misled their people, and tried to bluff the entire world. The statements of Kaoukji were bombastic and usually very far removed from the realities of the situation. The threats to the Jews turned out to be empty, and even hollower were the menaces to the Americans and the world in general. On the whole, I give most of these men the benefit of the doubt and record that they probably believed what they said. Kaoukji was perhaps quite sincere when he said he was quite ready and that he would be able to defeat the Jews, but his military thinking was behind the times. He still fought battles with rifles and small bands hidden behind the barren rocks of the Palestinian hills when the Israelis were thinking in terms of planes, radios, mechanized units, and tough striking forces.

Haj Amin el Husseini, whom I had often met in Cairo and other capitals of the Middle East, was not of those who spoke a great deal. He had always preferred to move and operate silently. He never even told his best friends when he was about to travel and used to arrive and depart mysteriously. He was the same in his speeches and interviews, cloaking his words in mystery, smiling mystically through his reddish, greying beard, with blue eyes either twinkling mischievously or narrowing ominously. He hardly ever spoke of his own personal life or plans, but his main theme, whenever he spoke to me, consisted of warning the United States not to support Israel against the Arab and Muslim worlds.

"The United States are liked in this part of the world. We still have pleasant memories of what they brought us during the tragic days that followed the First World War. Then, our people were starving and America brought us relief workers and food. American schools, hospitals, and universities are popular, respected institutions in the Arab Near East. When you write, tell the Americans not to mar this record."

Once as I sat with Mufti, I told him frankly that the Americans were highly critical of him because he had gone over to the Axis camp during the war and that he was considered undemocratic.

"I was pushed into the Axis camp by the steady refusal of Britain to ever allow my people to enjoy the privileges of democracy. They betrayed us from the very start and stripped us of every right. The British might be democratic in their own country, but we saw nothing of this democracy in the way they treated us.''

Mufti Effendi, as his followers called him, said that he never went straight to Germany but kept trying to avoid the British who were after him. From Palestine, he went to French-controlled Lebanon, and when the British made it too hot for him there, he left for Iraq. From there he went to Iran, and when the Russians and the British started closing in on this country and Anthony Eden was telling the House of Commons that the trap was closing in on the mufti, he managed to escape to Axis Europe.

But even the mufti, in talking about the Jews, claimed he would be able to dispose of them without any trouble. Neither he nor any other Arab leader tried to reach any understanding with the world powers over Palestine. Almost every suggestion put forward over Palestine was rejected by the Arabs, and the blasts of defiance against the world continued. Late in February 1948, I went to see the then Lebanese prime minister, Riad Solh Bey, who was assassinated in 1951. Solh had just returned to Beirut from Cairo, where he had presided at the Arab League sessions there in which the Palestine question and the U.N. debates on the Holy Land had been discussed.

At that time, Solh was feeling expansive. This was his normal mood, and that day he surpassed himself. I asked him whether he was talking on or off the record, and he said, ''You can use it all.'' He started dictating, and I am repeating his words to show the trend of thinking and the speeches that were then quite common.

''Every American interest throughout the Middle East will suffer if the United States continue to support the partition of Palestine,'' said Solh. He said that the Arab states had unanimously decided to reject any request to allow the Americans to build a pipeline from Saudi Arabia, passing through any Arab country. Solh said: ''The pipeline engineers had originally thought of building their line through Syria and Lebanon, but when they saw we refused, they threatened us by stating they would pass through Transjordan and Egypt. At the Arab League sessions, we were all united to reject the pipeline. We will continue to reject or spike every American interest in the Middle East so long as the Americans persist in partitioning Palestine."

This meeting with Solh coincided with the beginning of the Security Council debate on Palestine, and Solh commented, "We are prepared for the worst. We have tackled every possibility, even the possibility of the United Nations sending an international army to impose partition and to occupy the Holy Land. I would not worry if they send 100,000 men tomorrow. How long will the Guatemalans or the Nicaraguans remain in Palestine to defend a Jewish state? We will keep up our campaign despite foreign occupation. When these forces go we will still be fighting for Palestine's freedom. The world must realize that every Arab considers Palestine his fight.

"The independence of every Arab state is violated when the sovereignty of Arab Palestine is violated. The foreign occupation of Haifa is as much an attack against the Lebanese as the occupation of Beirut. Jaffa is as much Egypt's concern as Alexandria. The Lebanese, Egyptians, and other Arabs will fight to defend these Palestinian towns as much as their own cities. Americans, especially, must realise that every interest they have got is threatened throughout the Middle East if they continue to pursue this policy. We have spoken until we are hoarse. Now we have got no other way except to defend our soil with our blood. The United Nations must place at least one foreign soldier for every Jew in Palestine to defend them. I am not bluffing when I say that we are willing to die for Palestine."

Whether he realized it then or not, this speech was a bluff. Neither did the American oil interests nor any other American interests suffer more than a momentary embarrassment, nor did many Arabs feel really inclined to die for Palestine, especially with the lack of equipment. But these speeches and others more fiery hammered at the Arabs daily by their leaders left their mark on the masses. Their hatred of America and the West in general grew. They became convinced they were strong and would be able to hold out for long against the entire world if necessary. So, in the beginning, with such speeches stirring them on, the Arabs went ahead with their Jihad against the Jews in Palestine. I learned that Kaoukji would not enter Palestine until the Security Council sessions had ended and that, for the moment, only small raids would be carried out against the Jews.

For lack of something better to do, and because it was a story that had not yet been written, I decided to try to join the Arabs who were already in Palestine. Again I set off from Beirut and headed for Marjeyoun. From there, I contacted the people I had befriended at the border on my last trip, and they advised what route I should take. Right on the frontier a young volunteer offered to guide me to the area commander.

"Do I leave my car here?" I asked. The volunteer, who hailed from the town of Homs in Syria, answered, "You can drive practically anywhere in this area, especially in daytime. At night, it is dangerous because we shoot at cars. That's when the Jews try to sneak convoys with supplies to their settlements."

We drove into Palestine across an area of Northern Galilee that was dotted with roadblocks and barbed wire, previously manned by the British and now deserted. As we neared Arab villages in the area, we had to slow down to wind our way through the rocks that were purposely thrown across the road. Seoud, my guide, waved to the villagers as we drove by and kept up a steady stream of comment, pointing out various Jewish settlements a few miles away and telling me of the raids on which he had gone.

Seoud was nineteen years old and had been in Palestine for three months. "So far it has been child's play. There have been no attacks worthy of real men. We have been shooting guns, sniping, and ambushing convoys. But wars differ today to those of our forefathers. There is so much politics mingled with the fighting. We can easily destroy these settlements, but our commanders tell us the time is not yet come for action.''

To Seoud, battles were clashes on horseback and swords gleaming in the sun. I could imagine him sitting around a campfire back among his wide-eyed tribesmen listening to the tales the older men recounted of tribal wars in the desert. He had come to Palestine, a gun in his hand. Later, near Safad, he died, and survivors of the battle told me of that bewildered desert youth, dazed by aerial bombardment and shells fired at him by unseen foes, again saying, ''This is not a war of men.'' He died without fear of death but confused because he did not know how to fight that day.

As we turned a corner on this twisting mountain road, I jammed my brakes as we saw a roadblock behind which were several armed men. They were members of the ''Yarmuk'' contingent of the Arab Army of Liberation. Seoud jumped out and identified us, and the men surrounded the car and welcomed us. An officer, a blue-eyed Syrian in his late forties, appeared and greeted me. He wore a British army battle dress with a Bedouin kuffieh on his head. A warm sheepskin coat covered his uniform. Palestine was having one of its coldest winters, and the snows had covered the Gallilean hills.

This officer was in a hurry as he had an appointment with one Col. Adib el Shishakly, the commander of this area. I asked whether I could follow him and, on being granted permission, I trailed behind the truck on which was the officer and three younger lieutenants. Seoud kept telling me stories. He told me that Shishakly was one of the leaders on this front; in fact, Kaoukji's deputy. He was a lieutenant colonel in the Syrian army but had resigned to fight in Palestine.

But Seoud was more interested in telling me stories of battles. I rather suspected he was rehearsing on me what he hoped to tell around the campfire when he got back home. He told me the story of how Jewesses fought harder and better than Jews in one battle:

"A few days ago a Jewish patrol attacked an Arab bus in this area in one of their rare sorties nowadays. A Jewess tossed an incendiary bomb and set the bus on fire. Four Arabs were burned to death, but three other occupants threw themselves out into a ditch by the side of the road. Only the Arab driver was armed with a pistol, and as he peered over the edge of the ditch, he saw the Jewess, armed with a Sten gun, advancing towards them, firing a few rounds. Behind her were two Jews with tommy guns. Luck was with the Arab driver. A gust of wind blew the girl's long hair over her eyes. She raised a hand to brush back her hair, and quickly the Arab driver raised his head and squeezed the trigger. The girl dropped dead. The two men behind her turned and ran. They are devils, those women."

But that time, we had reached a little village, where about one hundred men were stationed. Inside the mukhtar's (mayor's) house, various Arab officers were conferring with Shishakly. Armed villagers stood guard behind sandbagged roofs. Some had daggers or grenades strapped to their waists. Most of them wore sheepskin coats to warm them against the biting cold and had covered their faces with their woollen kuffieh.

The Arabs gathered around us, the latest arrivals from the outside world, to get news of developments abroad. They offered me the bitter, spiced coffee of the Bedouins, and we squatted around, waiting for the commanders to finish their conference.

Adib el Shishakly was a small, soft-spoken man with a black beard streaked with grey. I was introduced to this commander of the Arab forces, who was in charge of the area stretching roughly from the Syro-Lebanese frontier to Tiberias and from there to Acre. Little was I then to know that Shishakly was going to figure prominently in a series of dramatic coups d'état in Syria and end up in 1951 by being the unchallenged strongman of his country. He was later assassinated in Brazil.

He received me in the mukhtar's house, and he sat there surrounded by his staff of youthful officers. Most of them had grown beards. Shishakly explained to me that his force, the first to enter Palestine, had been operating for three months already.

"We carry out an average of six daily attacks in which we usually kill a couple of Jews and wound half a dozen. Our aim is to discover the strength of the Jews and their equipment and to cut their routes. We have prevented supplies reaching their settlements. At times when they have been short of supplies, they have asked planes to drop supplies or have been obliged to request help from the British."

Shishakly told me he had commanded a raid on Yethyiam where only the arrival of British troops saved the Jews from annihilation. He explained to me that he was making a quick tour of inspection of his area, and I accompanied him through several villages.

In one of them we had lunch with the mukhtar. We all sat cross-legged on cushions and ate out of dishes placed on a low table between us. The officers sat around the table while in the background hovered the armed village notables whose guests we were. We scooped our food with the soft, thin bread from the dishes in the middle of the table. There were no plates in front of us. As I ate, I examined Shishakly. He had served with the French army in the Levant, and over his khaki uniform he wore a long blue cape, clasped around his neck. He never raised his voice, but spoke in low, clear tones, whether he was addressing me or his subalterns.

"We have examined the Jewish settlements very carefully and all of them have been built on easily defensible positions. The Jews have picked their sites well and have good equipment, such as mortars, machine guns, grenades, and to those they have added three-inch guns. Most of their ammunition is manufactured locally, somewhere south of Tiberias. They maintain wireless contact between each settlement.'' I thought of young Seoud outside, who, simple tribesman that he was, thought the settlements would be a pushover. What impressed me most about Shishakly was that for the first time I was hearing somebody making sense. He was a real soldier who knew his job and the difficulties ahead. There was none of the brash confidence of the others who thought the whole thing was just too easy for words.

He was, however, confident that when the time came he could occupy the Jewish settlements, given the necessary equipment. ''I believe I can take any Jewish settlement here in ten hours.''

After lunch he gave the gathered villagers a pep talk and then hopped into his jeep, and with a curt wave of his hand, swirled away to the cries of ''Go in Allah's safekeeping.''

I spent the night among these people, and I must confess I have slept in better beds, but I could not complain. The next day I wandered around some more, photographing the Arab fighters, visiting some of their furthermost points, and talking to the men. That afternoon, I set off for Beirut with all the material I had gathered. I had not filed any stories for two or three days, and there was no sense in sitting on the material I had obtained.

You shoot first and ask questions later at night in Palestine. Without the guides offered to me by the local commanders, I would have been a dead duck travelling in the threatening darkness of the Holy Land. As I drove back towards the Lebanese frontier, the sun was setting. Night sets in quickly in the Middle East and before long we were in complete darkness. Just about that time I arrived to a little mountain village where another unit of the Yarmouk contingent was billeted. The local commander greeted me, provided me with gas for my car, but warned me, ''If you want to go on, I must warn you the road is dangerous. You had better spend the night here and proceed next morning. The Jews sometimes organize raiding parties at night, so we usually shoot first and ask questions later whenever anyone approaches our villages.''

I preferred to continue my journey, so he provided me with guides who were to use prearranged signals to prevent the Arabs from firing at us. We drove along the bumpy road until we came to roadblocks behind which were Arab sentries mounting guard. They flagged us down and checked our identities. Other Arabs were silhouetted behind the rocks on the hillsides, their rifles cautiously pointing at us. They were taking no chances at being caught unaware by Jews. One of the sentries explained, pointing to lights in the distance: ``These are three Jewish settlements. They are short of supplies, and at night they might either attempt to raid our villages or sneak through a convoy. We must be prepared for them.''

As we drove on, I must confess I was not feeling very happy. I was more worried about Arabs mistaking us for a Jewish car, than I was of a Jewish raid. My guides sat tensely as the car drove on. They were more used to crawling over the hills than motoring over roads, and they knew what an attractive target the headlights made to their trigger-happy comrades. We were challenged four times on our trip, and when we finally reached the Lebanese frontier, the guides were very relieved to get rid of me.

This was the situation during the few months that preceded the final departure of the British forces from Palestine. Kaoukji entered Palestine in the early days of March and was at first satisfied to harass Jewish convoys and consolidate his ``Triangle of Terror,'' situated in the Nablus-Jenin-Tulkarm area. From there he tried to attack the strategic Jewish stronghold of Mishmar ha Emek, the Armageddon of Biblical days, and almost got his entire force wiped out. At that time, the Jews proved they were redoubtable fighters, and the Kaoukji reputation suffered its first setback.

Still, the Arabs were overconfident and such leading figures as Ahmed Sharabaty, Syrian minister of national defence and considered one of the most active persons in the entire Arab movement, kept making cheerful statements that later turned out to be completely untrue. I went back to Damascus to see what was happening there, and I asked to meet Sharabaty, who was supposed to be masterminding the entire campaign. It was not easy to meet him, but once I had managed that, he had a good deal to say. He outlined the situation and started off by saying that the Arabs will be using more men and better arms than the Jews in the Palestine battle.

"We have taken the maximum figures which the Jews are supposed to have and topped this by several thousands. The Jews claim they have seventy thousand trained fighters. We know this is a myth, but we have accepted this number and then built up an army exceeding this figure. We know what arms the Zionists have got and we have obtained superior weapons with which to fight them."

Sharabaty spoke well, and his rugged face and coal black eyes were very expressive as he smoothly continued, "Volunteers have poured in from every Arab country. There have been so many that we have turned back thousands. We have picked all we need. Less than one-fourth of our total Arab Army of Liberation is at present in Palestine. We are holding back more than three-quarters for future operations."

He said that the Arab forces were trying to avoid a clash with the British as they had no quarrel with them. In fact, he said, the British were wise enough not to support the partition scheme which was discussed at the United Nations. He predicted that when the British finally withdraw from Palestine, the "big fight" would start. He said much more during this meeting. Like, for example, "No Arab soldier, wherever he may be fighting, will run short of either rations or ammunition. All requirements will be fulfilled according to schedule."

Not much later, in Amman, Transjordan, I sat beside Gen. Ismail Safwat Pasha, the Iraqi supreme commander of the Arab Army of Liberation, and listened to a conversation between him and some Palestinian Arab volunteers who had come from one of the strife-torn areas. They told him that from their sector they often helplessly watched Jewish convoys pass without being able to do anything about it.

General Safwat raised his beetling eyebrows and growled, "Why?"

"Because our ammunition had run out and all we could do was hide and hope the Jews wouldn't attack us."

The gruff old warrior, perhaps a brave man, but scarcely the ideal commander for the twentieth century, looked at them contemptuously and said, "This is not the talk of men, but of chickenhearted weaklings. When you have no bullets left, you throw stones and fight with your bare hands."

"Against armored cars, General?" asked one of the Palestinians.

"Yes," shouted Safwat, "against armored cars." Those men had come to appeal for more arms and went back empty-handed. I thought of the confidence of Sharabaty just a few days back and wondered who he was fooling—himself, his people, or the outside world.

The only man who struck a warning note at a time when all were optimistically predicting the lightning defeat of the Jews once the British were out of the country was the Arab League's secretary-general, Abdel Rahman Azzam Pasha. He came over to Beirut for a meeting of the Arab League's political committee and told me, "The Jews are still stronger than the Arabs in Palestine. I am confident of the final Arab victory, but the Jews have years of organisation and possess a well-trained striking force. They have fortified areas that are easily defensible. On the Arab side, there is excellent morale, time, and numbers." I told him of some of the statements that other Arab leaders had made to me—that the Arabs were even at that time stronger than the Jews. He shook his head in exasperation.

Meanwhile, in the United Nations, the Arabs were taking a political beating. Arab infiltration into Palestine was considered a threat to peace. Even Russia sided with the West on this issue—probably the first time that the Russians and the West had ever agreed on anything in the post-world war era.

Throughout the Middle East, resentment against the United States was increasing as more prominent Americans kept making pro-Zionist statements. Nobody seemed even conscious of the fact that Arabs existed or had any rights in Palestine.

Answering UN accusations that the infiltration of Arab volunteers constituted a threat to world peace, Azzam snapped back: "No more than the entry of Jewish immigrants who are picked young and able-bodied. Why don't the powers consider Jewish infiltration a threat to peace?"

At that time, the United States had effected a *volte-face*, proposed the scrapping of the partition proposals and the establishment of a temporary U.N. trusteeship over Palestine. This announcement came just at the time when the Arab League, meeting in Beirut, was celebrating its third anniversary. The Arabs were delighted, and each leader was loud in his praise of the Americans. Matters looked bright for the future and Arab leaders predicted that a great Arab-American alliance would soon result.

Arab leaders celebrated the third anniversary of the League with heightened enthusiasm following the United States proposal to junk the Palestine partition scheme. The sudden American *volte-face* had boosted the League's prestige among the masses and paved the way for greater cooperation with the West on two major scores—anti-communism and oil. While the Arab governments were by their very nature anti-communists, Anglo-American policy had driven considerable numbers of the masses towards communism.

But this American *volte-face* was destined to be very short-lived, and another dramatic turn was to take place again, this time against the Arabs.

Meanwhile, in Palestine, clashes between the Jews and Arabs were increasing, and fairly large forces were fighting each other. By April 1948, there were many fewer British soldiers in many parts of Palestine, and the Jews and Arabs were often at each others' throats. By that time, too, the Arabs had found that the Jews were not going to be as easy to liquidate as they had anticipated.

A conference took place in Damascus bringing together all the commanders of the various Arab volunteer forces in Palestine with several political leaders including Haj el Husseini. There had been a reversal on the Jerusalem front where the Jews had captured Kastel, a key village on the Jerusalem-Tel Aviv route.

The commander of the Jerusalem front, Abdel Kader el Husseini, was conferring with the mufti and Generals Safwat and Hashimi. He gave them a report on the situation and helped them draw up plans to retake the village. Abdel Kader was a young man, educated at the American University in Cairo, and had always been a great believer in the Arab cause in Palestine. He had three young sons when he volunteered to lead the Arab forces in Jerusalem. I saw him when he reached the Orient Palace Hotel in Damascus. He was still wearing the shabby clothes in which he fought in the hills around the city. Under his sweater, the muzzle of a revolver jutted out, and his shoes were muddy. He obviously had had little sleep recently and was impatient. He told his two bodyguards in low, impatient tones, "We are wasting time here." He had just finished some meetings, and it seemed that he was anxious to get back to his fighters. He was very confident of the future and felt sure the Arabs would ultimately beat the Jews.

"I am going to Palestine, and my actions will speak louder than my words," he told me. "Look me up at my headquarters at Abou Zeid, near Jerusalem, and I will show you deeds rather than words." When he smiled, there was a gap in his mouth where two front teeth had been knocked out. He talked to me about Palestine and, like most other Arabs, commented on the American policy. That same night, he left for Palestine with plans to immediately attack and take Kastel. He was killed the following day, leading his men in an attack against this vital village.

Abdel Kader had often been urged by his friends not to expose himself so often to danger. As a leader of a front, they told him he should not personally lead attacks against the enemy but should direct the battle.

I received the news in Damascus of Abdel Kader's death before the Arab high commander did, and this was a sorry comment on their organisation. When the news reached me, I went round to see the mufti's entourage, and they had had no information on the matter. All they knew was that a battle was going on for Kastel. They immediately sent a message to Jerusalem. Within a few moments, there were dozens of people anxiously crowding the mufti's room, waiting for news of Abdel Kader.

After a lengthy delay, a message reached the mufti that his nephew Abdel Kader had died in battle. He turned a grave face to the people around him and said, "I offer you condolences on the death of a fighter of the Jihad." This was his way of showing that Abdel Kader was not merely a member of his family but belonged to all the Arabs. Then the mufti continued smilingly, "We should not be dismayed by his death. Rather, we should congratulate ourselves on the way he died."

Many of the men around Haj Amin cried openly, but he remained very calm, even comforting the people around him.

During the next few weeks, I spent most of my time shuttling back and forth between various Arab capitals and different parts of Palestine. A quick trip to Northern Palestine showed more Arab irregulars had gone in and established strong points close to the sea to cut the coastal roads just as soon as the British stopped using them. The Jews were also getting ready. Arab scouts in the area of Safad and the Jewish settlements in Galilee and the Tiberias region said the Jews were very strong in the area and were determined to hold.

To travel between Haifa and Beirut became a major hazard with both Jews and Arabs shooting up convoys on the road. Reporters often had to move with an escort of British armored cars to get through various danger zones. At other times, it was just impossible to get through until the two stopped fighting for a while.

There were many colorful stories. In many ways, the mounting war was becoming more than just a straight fight between Arabs and Jews. There were volunteers rolling in from various corners of the globe. There were soldiers of fortune, idealists, and those with an axe to grind. Both on the Jewish and Arab sides, there were reports of foreign volunteers. In Beirut, I had seen some Germans, former officers in the Nazi Army, who had come out to offer their services to the Arabs. Some of these were prompted by their hatred of the Jews, others because they knew no other profession but fighting, and still more were escaped prisoners of war who had slipped out of the British camps in the Suez Canal zone.

There were Yugoslavs. Some were Muslim Ustachis who had fought with the Germans during the World War II under Pavlevitch. There were other Yugoslavs who had either fought with Mikhailovitch and now were living in exile in the Middle East, or who had come out of Yugoslavia with King Peter and now wanted a job.

At Deraa, the Syrian frontier town just before Transjordan, I ran into a truckload of armed youths, wearing the Bedouin kuffieh and khaki uniforms. They were obviously members of the Arab volunteer forces on their way into Transjordan and, thence, to one of the fronts. It was a fairly common sight in

Deraa, but as I passed them, I saw one spit out his food and mutter in unmistakable English: "I can't eat that bloody stuff." Four other English voices echoed his sentiments from behind their Arab headgear.

There were English deserters from the British army who had joined the Arabs to fight the Jews. As the British were evacuating the Holy Land, the soldiers escaped and sought shelter with the Arabs. They were now reentering Palestine to fight. Three of these youths came from Liverpool, one from Northern Ireland, and the other from Manchester. I never got their names because their Arab commander, Major Mahmoud Rifai, the Potsdam-trained aide of Kaoukji, ordered them to keep quiet.

One of them wanted permission to give me a cable to send to his girl back home, but a grey-haired Arab security officer told him that all the messages must go through the regular military channels. I asked the Englishman why they had wanted to fight the Jews, and they answered that the Jewish terrorists had killed some of their comrades, and they were out to avenge them. One of the Liverpool men told me that Jews had killed three of his friends and wounded him, and he had sworn he would get even with them.

They were all carrying rifles, and the British had added commando knives to their belts. The Manchester youth, who had spat out the contents of the sandwich that the villagers had offered him, said, "Most of the food we get here is all right, but I can't stomach this sour milk they like and that sandwich contained just that."

Around the middle of April, there were more political meetings, and by now there were some references to King Abdullah and his Arab Legion of Transjordan. Although no one admitted it, the Arabs were starting to find that unless they got the support of a regular trained army, they would not have an easy time. Kaoukji went to Amman, secretly at first, and then openly, and reports indicated he had obtained the promise of artillery and mechanized support from King Abdullah.

At that time, Haifa fell to the Jews. The British suddenly decided to evacuate all but the port area of this vital city, and the Jewish forces, better prepared and led, swooped throught the town and captured it after some bitter street fighting. The Arabs were caught by surprise, and their uncoordinated resistance collapsed in front of the Jewish assaults. Throughout the Arab world, there were bitter attacks against the British, with people accusing them of having warned the Jews they were clearing out of the town. This, say the Arabs, gave the Jews the necessary time to organise their occupation of the city. The Hagana, the Jewish force, was soon in control of the town, and the considerable Arab population was in flight.

Those that could came by road. But most sought refuge in the coastal strip and were brought out by a fleet of fishing smacks, schooners, and sailing vessels that Lebanon sent to evacuate the Arabs. For days, a little Dunkirk took place. Tyre became a refugee centre for the Haifa population.

The Haifa incident showed up the Arab Army of Liberation. The truth exploded with startling clarity. They were not as numerous as they had claimed to be. They were not properly equipped, and they were not properly led. Every Arab newspaper started screaming that the regular Arab armies must now step in before a worse disaster hit the Arabs.

Overnight, Amman, the small capital of Transjordan, became the scene of military meetings and the centre of Arab activity. While the Arabs had previously tended to ignore King Abdullah and concentrated on the mufti, now the tables were turned. The mufti's men had failed in Haifa, and the Damascus organisation was obviously very poor. Transjordan and Iraq, formerly considered British puppets that should not take a leading role in the Palestine affair, suddenly became the hopes of the Arab world. Many of the Arabs who had previously feared that King

Abdullah's participation would mean his automatic annexation of Palestine said, "Better to have Palestine under King Abdullah, and even Syria and Lebanon under him, than to have the Jews rule the Holy Land."

By the beginning of April, as the deadline approached, King Abdullah of Transjordan held the stage. All eyes in the Arab world turned to him. In Raghdan Palace overlooking his ancient capital of Amman, the Philadelphia of the Romans, the bearded monarch saw with grim satisfaction the leaders of the Arab world flocking to his doorstep and praising his well-trained, mechanized Arab Legion. After having accused the Arab Legion of being a British tool, the mercurial Arabs agreed that it was the only hope for an Arab victory in Palestine.

The developments were, to King Abdullah, a justification of his persistently pro-British policy over a long number of years. While others had condemned his attitude, he had claimed that in the long run his alliance with Britain would serve his and the Arabs' interests best. In his mind, there were never any differences between himself and the Arabs in general. That day, when the Arab leaders came flocking to hail him, was Abdullah's day.

I had often had audiences with King Abdullah. He was a very modest man and usually very easy to meet. He had granted me an occasional interview, but more often he had just been pleased to talk "off the record."

"If you print a word of what I have told you, I shall just deny it," he would warn me quite simply when he did not want his words quoted.

During the early days of the Palestine preparations, when most of the Arab leaders tended to ignore King Abdullah, I had gone to see him. He had been very contemptuous of those he called the "Damascus crowd," and criticized their plans. He thought they were going about their preparations in a very amateurish way, not at all keeping with the times.

"The days of fighting with bows and arrows, with spears and with men on horses firing rifles is gone. Today, armies must have technical training, mechanized units, and maximum efficiency to strike effectively. This is the kind of army I have got," said the king. He was proud of his British-trained legion, and despite his own very Oriental, conservative way of life, he was well aware that change was essential. His first move had been to modernize the army.

His friends and his courtiers claimed with pride he had proven himself to be much more farsighted that any of the other Arab leaders. One of them told me, "He tackled realistically the problems of the Arab world. You cannot oppose and fight all the great powers. If we combat communism, then we must befriend the British or the Americans. If we want to improve our technical skills, we must not be ashamed to learn and benefit from others."

King Abdullah had also told me the same thing but had cautiously added that while he wanted his subjects to learn from the West, he urged them to be able to distinguish the good from the bad. "Let them learn and adopt all the good the West can provide and add it to the good they have inherited from their fathers. But they must not fall prey to many of the evils that grip the West. Should their search be deep, they will find many things they can learn from the West and adapt to our way of life. If they are superficial in their quest, they will merely add Western evils to the undeniable evils that even now curse the Arab world."

Even before the fall of Haifa to the Hagana, King Abdullah had predicted to me that the Arab volunteers and the Palestine Arabs, organized as they were, could not cope with the Zionists. "What you need are trained forces and men used to modern weapons." After the fall of Haifa, and the subsequent loss of considerable portions of Palestine to the Jews, King Abdullah was sad, but he could not hide a grim satisfaction that the turn of events had justified his predictions.

Overnight, Amman replaced Damascus as the military capital of the Arab world. King Abdullah was named supreme commander of the Arab forces which were going to enter Palestine once the British had evacuated. It was understood that these forces would be spearheaded by the Arab Legion.

Gen. Ismail Safwat, commander of the Arab Army of Liberation, came to Amman and told newspapermen that the fighting had entered a new phase demanding the participation of the regular armies of the Arab world. "We need regulars. Our volunteers are insufficiently trained and were only useful to gain time. If regular armies cannot be sent from those states who are members of the United Nations, then they must be released in order to join the Arab Legion." Transjordan was not a member of the United Nations organisation and could therefore act without fear of violating any international agreement.

Azzam Pasha came to Amman to confer with Abdullah. From Iraq, the king's nephew Regent Abdul Ilah also arrived. Simultaneously, came the announcement that Iraqi troops were already moving across the desert towards Transjordan where they would join the Arab Legion for the coming fight.

Other Arab leaders flocked to Amman, Premier Riad Solh of Lebanon, Syria's Jamil Mardam, senior officers of the Egyptian, Iraqi, Syrian, and Lebanese armies came over as well as the Syrian and Lebanese defence ministers.

At that time, it was decided that the regular armies should do no more than occupy various Arab parts of Palestine, and not to attack the Jews. Guerilla forces would then be sent into the Jewish parts of the Holy Land. By that time, the Arab leaders had decided that silence was perhaps a wiser course than the optimistic declarations they had previously been inclined to make. It was very difficult to get anything out of them, but I understood from some of the delegation members whom I had known intimately in the past that there was no question of an all-out assault against the Jews. The Arabs now realised that it would need tens of thousands of well-trained, well-equipped forces to carry out any major military invasion, and they did not possess such forces.

They, therefore, decided on a war of attrition after May 15, and politically, they all accepted the likelihood of King Abdullah annexing the Arab part of Palestine, although there might be some opposition made by some states.

At the same time, in Amman there were already rumors that King Abdullah would seek an understanding with the Jews, providing they would accept certain basic conditions, the principal one being a limited immigration.

But matters were moving very fast and policies likely to change every day. With the tremendous activity in Amman, this tiny capital of a country that all in all numbered about four hundred thousand became one of the busiest spots in the world. Correspondents converged into the town from the four corners of the globe. But it was still very difficult to send out any news as Amman did not have adequate means for cable transmission. News dispatches were telephoned through to Damascus or Beirut, or put on planes heading for Cairo. Sometimes, newsmen managed to get in touch with their Jerusalem colleagues and dictate or hand them messages for transmission from there.

May 1: Only a fortnight to go before the British finally washed their hands of the Palestine affair. In Amman, correspondents were trying to find accomodations in a town that boasted of only one hotel and a few apologies for hotels. At the Philadelphia Hotel, newsmen crowded four and five per room.

At dawn that day, I went over to Raghdan Palace in the hope of being received by King Abdullah. As usual, after his early morning prayers, he liked to walk through his garden and sit in a little outhouse to sip coffee with his chamberlain. One of his Circassian guards led me to the king. As usual, we spent a few moments exchanging greetings and sipping coffee. The king always began by discussing world affairs. I used to wait for a signal from his secretary to ask my questions. Sometimes when the king was in a bad mood, it was better not to seek answers. That day, however, although in a grim mood, he seemed disposed to talk.

He confirmed that Arab forces from neighboring states would reinforce the Palestinian Arabs as soon as the British troops departed and Britain's mandate over Palestine ended. "We are grimly awaiting the departure of Britain, and then we will go into Palestine to help our Arab brothers there, with God's help," he declared. "The situation is very critical. The most dangerous time will be between the departure of the British and the arrival of our forces in Jerusalem. The Holy Places are threatened. Our task will not be easy. While the United Nations sit and confer, we in Amman are preparing to act. I believe the Jews will attempt to seize all of Palestine so long as they find no effective opposition to their forces. We are justified both on humanitarian and political grounds to enter Palestine and protect the Arabs."

He paused for a while, and then said, "What is happening and what will happen in Palestine may be the spark that will set the whole world aflame. A United Nations commission has sent me a message urging that I stop my forces from entering Palestine, alleging that this would be a threat to security. Security ended when the Jews shot the British high commissioner in Palestine (Sir Harold MacMichael), when they murdered the British minister of state (Lord Moyne, in Cairo), when they strung up British soldiers, and when they murdered whole Arab villages."

The king said some more, and throughout, he spoke with more emotion than I had been accustomed to hear from him. "We have no wish to persecute the Jews, but we cannot allow the Arabs to be persecuted," he said. A photographer who accompanied me that day asked the king to pose for a few pictures. The bearded monarch looked gravely at the camera as the flashlights exploded. The photographer asked me to persuade the king to smile. With good grace, the king flashed a smile and then turned towards me and said sadly, "My smile does not come from my heart." Little did he know that, as a result of the Palestine war and in the Holy Places he was so anxious to defend, he would later be shot and killed by some Palestinian Arabs who blamed their sorry state on him.

As the days went by, there were more troops movements and several clashes between the Jews and Arabs in various sectors. The British did not interfere anymore, so long as they did not interfere with any evacuation plans. In Northern Palestine, Safad fell to the Jews after a long and bitter fight. Thus, almost all the major towns of Palestine had now fallen into Zionist hands, with the exception of those in the south.

With May 15 only a couple of days away, Jean Nieuwenhuys, Belgian consul-general in Jerusalem and chairman of the Security Council's Truce Commission, came to Amman with Dr. Pablo Azcarate, Trygvie Lie's personal envoy to Palestine. They were received in audience by King Abdullah and discussed with him the possibility of reaching a truce for Jerusalem. The world in general wanted to save Jerusalem from destruction. The meeting was not very conclusive.

Arab military leaders were now in full strength in Amman, working out the last details of the campaign that would start as of May 15. As it turned out, they prepared a sound plan of campaign, both from a military and political viewpoint, but at the last minute each abandoned the proposed coordinated action and went ahead with a different idea which turned out to be disastrous for them.

At their last meeting in Amman, the military leaders, along with the politicians, had agreed that they would have about three weeks in which to gain the upper hand in Palestine and hold a bargaining position. Reports from Lake Success clearly showed them that the United Nations would not allow a long war in the Holy Land. It was felt that between three to four weeks would elapse before the Security Council stepped in and forced the fighting to stop. It was therefore essential, argued the Arab leaders, to be in a good bargaining position at the end of that time.

The plan roughly was for the Egyptian commandos and the Arab Legion of Transjordan to encircle Jerusalem, without trying to enter the Jewish held part of the city. The Iraqi force, which was to cut the Haifa road, would also head for Tel Aviv. Thus the Arabs would be advancing from every direction on the then Jewish "capital." With Jerusalem surrounded, Tel Aviv encircled, Haifa cut off from the hinterland by the Syrian, Lebanese, and Kaoukji forces, the Arabs would have been in a good bargaining position when the United Nations forced a truce.

As it turned out, just as soon as May 15 arrived, every Arab government switched to another plan, for a variety of reasons, and any hope of being in a good bargaining position when the truce came was destroyed.

For sentimental reasons, King Abdullah ordered his troops to move into Jerusalem. He feared his father's tomb would fall into Jewish hands, as the Israelis in Jerusalem were pressing hard against the Palestinian Arabs defending the Old City. The Arab Legion lost a comparatively heavy number of men in the street fighting to which they were not used.

The Egyptians were not able to send as many men and as much equipment as they should have into the battle, and this slowed down their advance along the coast towards Tel Aviv.

The Iraqi commanders changed their minds about cutting the Haifa-Tel Aviv road and about advancing towards Tel Aviv. They decided instead to strike for the port of Haifa itself, which was the terminal point of their Iraqi pipeline, and where Iraqi oil was refined. They bogged down right from the start in front of a few well-defended, strategically-placed settlements.

The Syrians, who were supposed to join the Lebanese in occupying Acre and cutting Haifa from the hinterland, decided they would join the Iraqis in their bid for Haifa and got badly mauled at the frontier.

When the fighting came to an end about one month later, the Arabs did not have any really good bargaining position. True, they had advanced almost everywhere but not enough to hold the whip hand.

The four-week truce, which Count Folke Bernadotte, the Swedish mediator chosen by the United Nations, had persuaded both sides to accept, saw Jews and Arabs more or less holding their own.

The Egyptians held the Negev, in Southern Palestine, but there were Jewish settlements that were holding out although surrounded. The Zionists held all of Northern Palestine, which they had won from Kaoukji's forces. They also held a coastal strip running from Tel Aviv to the Lebanese frontier. The Iraqis were now holding the central part—Nablus, Jenin, Qalqilya, and Turkarm. The Transjordanians controlled Lydda and nearby Ramleh. The Jews held the new city of Jerusalem and the Arabs held the Old City.

Most of the Arab masses did not welcome this truce and urged their governments to keep on fighting. The governments, on the other hand, knew and feared possible United Nations sanctions and realized their own position was precarious, as they depended on equipment from abroad.

I paid another early morning visit to King Abdullah at his palace. I asked him to give me a statement for the United Press, commenting on the cease-fire and Count Bernadotte's mediation, scheduled to start on the Island of Rhodes.

"Will you write the truth?" asked the king. I assured the monarch that most correspondents had strict orders to report faithfully what they saw or heard and to be impartial in their stories.

"Write then what I have to say: We have avenged the people of Palestine from those who attacked their neighbors, despite their assertions that they were coming to live peacefully in a national home. This peace turned into clashes and chaos and the United Nations have told the Arabs who are the rightful owners.

Stop, otherwise I shall punish you economically, and I will take military measures against you. This is well known to all. The Arabs are not in a state of war with anybody, but there is in Palestine a fire which must be extinguished. The western states wish to bury this fire under embers which might rekindle and flame. If it does, it may lead to a new world war.

"This is what I say today. We in our country are ready to amalgamate the Jews into a Palestinian state in which they will enjoy full privileges, as the Arabs. They will have the administration they wish in their cities and settlements, except full sovereignty which is the right of the over-all Palestine Arab state. If the mediator succeeds in bringing this about, the Arabs are tolerant and forgiving, treating their neighbors amicably. If the Jews refuse, I am sure that no Arab state can feel secure with a hostile foreign state trying to grab all it can. The future will expose to the world what so far has been hidden."

This was King Abdullah's last word before the mediation started. Others said much more about it. Some predicted that it would be a failure; others believed that the United Nations would sell Palestine to the Jews. From a United Nations viewpoint, the four-week truce was a welcome period in which to try and settle matters peacefully. Fighting had not settled anything, and it did not look as though further clashes would lead to any concrete result.

The fighting was very confused and there were tremendous exaggerations in the communiqués issued by all sides. On the whole, the first month of war was very inconclusive and was more or less of a statemate. . . . It was evident, however, that the Israelis were not well prepared for the attacks of the Arab regular armies and did not possess enough equipment.

What they did not know at the time was that the Arabs themselves did not have much in reserve, and when both sides accepted the truce, it was because they did not have much choice in the matter. The man who dominated the scene at the time was Sweden's Count Folke Bernadotte. The eyes of the world followed this colorful personality whose only desire was to bring peace to a troubled section of the world.

From the battlefields of the Holy Land and the troubled cities of the Middle East, the scene shifted, for a few weeks, to the Island of Rhodes where the mission of the United Nations Mediator on Palestine established its headquarters in June of 1948.

XV
Rhodes—Mediation Island

Rhodes was a wonderful contrast to the battered cities of Palestine and the tense, riot-ridden Arab nations. The weather was perfect, the sea a beautiful blue, and the emphasis was on peace rather than war. The flag of the United Nations flew over the Hotel des Roses, a hotel that retained much of the luxury that had made it one of the pleasure palaces of Fascist Italy when Rhodes was a famous tourist resort and holiday playground for Fascist bigwigs.

Mussolini had ordered that the architecture of the island should preserve the style of the Crusaders whose knights of St. John had governed Rhodes for a period. There were castles and battlements, moats and drawbridges, narrow roads which took you past historic houses, and inns that had once been the homes of the French, English, Italian, German, and Spanish knights of St. John. There were slender minarets built by the Turks whose Suleiman the Magnificent had conquered the Knights, and the simple whitewashed churches of the Greek Orthodox inhabitants.

The Hotel des Roses was right on the beach. From the windows of our rooms, we could see the Taurus mountains of Turkey, rising in the distance, just across the few miles of sea that separated us from the Turkish mainland. On the beach were members of the United Nations, enjoying their off-duty hours, Greek tycoons, and honeymoon couples.

It was in this peaceful, lovely setting of that historic island that Count Folke Bernadotte was going to make his bid to settle the Palestine question. To his headquarters came correspondents from all parts of the world. Many who had covered the fighting, either from the Israeli or Arab side, came to the island.

Who was Count Bernadotte and his United Nations team? There were some names that had occasionally flitted through the front pages of the world's newspapers, but they were not very well known personalities. Bernadotte himself, of course, was the most prominent figure. But with him were other capable men. They were, for the most part, officials of the United Nations and army officers assigned to the mediator. Chiefly there was that interesting personality, Dr. Ralph Bunche, whose title then was "Personal Representative of the UN Secretary-General with Count Bernadotte and Chief of the United Nations Secretariat in Palestine."

The count was a blue-eyed, monocled Swedish aristocrat, a nephew of the king. His chief assistant was an American black, Bunche, who came from very humble stock. There was a French diplomat, Henri Vigier, a Greek, a South African, and a variety of lesser aides. Principally, however, it was the Bernadotte-Bunche combination that caught the public eye.

Bernadotte was born in Stockholm in 1895, the son of Prince Oscar, younger brother of King Gustav of Sweden. The count was educated in Swedish schools and then became a cavalry officer. In 1928, he married Estelle Manville of New York City in what was described as one of the most colorful marriages of a colorful decade. He had two sons, Ockie and Bertil. Countess Bernadotte and the two sons were with him on the island.

The count devoted most of his time to the Swedish Red Cross and the Swedish Boy Scouts. He was the head of the two organisations and the chairman of the Permanent Commission of the International Red Cross. During the Second World War, Bernadotte went to Paris in December 1944 and conducted discussions with the German authorities there, as a result of which he went to Germany in January 1945 to negotiate with Himmler the release of certain categories of people from Nazi concentration camps before the impending collapse of the Nazi regime.

As a result of these negotiations some twenty thousand Norwegians, Danes, Poles, Dutch, and Frenchwomen were released in early spring of 1945.

Ralph Bunche was born in Detroit in 1904 and was educated in public schools of Los Angeles. He took a number of degrees at the University of California and Harvard, including his Ph.D. in 1938. He became a professor of political science and chairman of the Department of Political Science at Harvard University and was granted leave of absence to undertake some responsible government jobs during and immediately after the war. He later became the director of the Department of Trusteeship of the United Nations.

Bernadotte worked cautiously from the start. He brought to Rhodes two delegations, one Jewish, one Arab, who could answer questions he might want to ask while preparing his suggestions for a permanent peace in Palestine. He did not tell them what he was trying to work out but just asked them questions on various aspects of the problem.

The truce had started on June 11, and by June 27, Bernadotte had produced some suggestions "as a possible basis for discussion." He entrusted his personal representatives to hand these over to both Jews and Arabs.

These suggestions did not form the total sum of his work. Bernadotte received daily reports from his observers in the field about the observance of the truce. There were complaints and minor crises that often took up much of his time.

On June 27, Bernadotte announced to the newsmen that his representatives had handed his suggestions to both sides: "I have asked both sides not to comment and not to make these suggestions public until I have received their first impressions."

The mediator said both Jews and Arabs would have the right to make countersuggestions. Bernadotte then started tackling various other problems—especially the Jerusalem situation.

He also had to take action on many incidents where both Arabs and Jews were flouting the authority of the United Nations, either deliberately or accidentally. His UN observers were constantly reporting accusations by both sides that the other was violating the truce agreement. Some cases were more serious than others and at times the entire truce was threatened by some of the problems that cropped up.

Bernadotte and his staff were faced daily with the problem of when it was wiser to be forceful or tactful. On the whole, Bernadotte was exploiting, to the greatest possible extent, the moral strength of the United Nations. He had no other weapons he could use, except perhaps his own strong personality.

To give an illustration of the type of incidents that went on, here are reports issued on July 1 following three incidents in late June, one on of the Jewish side and the other two on the Egyptian. They illustrate the difficulties and dangers under which the United Nations observers were forced to operate. Often the United Nations obtained little or no cooperation from the Arabs and Jews, while there were times when they were shot at, wounded, and killed by the trigger-happy soldiers of the various forces.

Incident in the Negev

Some time ago, Col. Thord Bonde, the mediator's deputy in charge of observing the truce in Palestine, informed the Egyptian commander in chief that supply convoys that were allowed to go to Jewish settlements in the Negev would be subject to the same regulations as convoys going to Jerusalem. In other words, the quantity of foodstuffs carried would be limited in such a way that the supply position at the end of the truce period would not be materially different than at the beginning of the truce. The convoys would be inspected by United Nations observers and would travel under United Nations authority.

On June 24, Colonel Bonde wrote to the Egyptian commander in chief and told him that on the following day, June 25, a convoy consisting of twenty-five Jewish trucks and three Jewish buses would leave for the Negev under United Nations escort and, in doing so, would pass through the Egyptian lines at a point southwest of Negba. The observers were to travel in jeeps that had been painted white and would carry a United Nations flag.

No reply had been received from the Egyptian commander by the morning of June 25, although the mediator in Rhodes, on the morning of June 25, did receive a message from the Egyptian authorities refusing to allow the convoy to pass. Having failed to receive a reply from the Egyptian commander, the observers proceeded to inspect the convoy south of Rehovat.

They were informed locally, on the morning of the 25, that passage would not be allowed and an observer reported that the crossroads at Negba were guarded by Egyptian armored cars while two Spitfires were in the air. They were also told that the brigadier who was in command had orders to stop the convoy.

Colonel Bonde, therefore, stopped the convoy before it came in sight of the Egyptian forces.

Spitfire Incident

On the same morning (June 25) Lt. Col. Michael Martin, United Nations observer (American), had been ordered to fly over the area around Negba in a light Auster observation plane. He reported that while he was flying near Negba, two Egyptian Spitfires came so close to him that the pilots were able to wave to one another. Martin's plane was painted white and had United Nations markings on both wings and the fuselage.

At 9:05 Martin landed behind the Jewish lines to refuel and report to Bonde. He reported that as he did so, and before the plane had stopped rolling, it was attacked by both Spitfires. The

Spitfires made four passes at the Auster while it was on the ground, Martin said. The Auster was hit 15 times.

There had been an understanding that the United Nations planes would normally fly at two thousand feet (as was subsequently pointed out by the Egyptian government in reply to Bernadotte's protest) but only when they were engaged in transport and Egyptian commanders had been informed that they would fly lower when on reconnaissance or engaged in ground observation.

After this incident, Colonel Bonde informed the Egyptian commander that he was withdrawing all United Nations observers from that particular sector because the United Nations flag was not being respected.

On June 26, Bernadotte informed the Egyptian government that he maintained his decision that passage of controlled food convoys to the Jewish settlements of the Negev was entirely in accord with the terms of the truce and he asked the Egyptian government to give him its final decision before Monday, June 28.

At the request of the Egyptian government, he extended this time by twenty-four hours.

On the evening of Monday, June 28, Dr. Pablo Ascarate, the mediator's representative in Cairo, was informed that the Egyptian government had decided to permit the passage of controlled food convoys to the Negev, in the interests of preserving the truce, while maintaining in principle its objection to such traffic, which it did not feel fell properly under Article 6, subparagraph 8 of the truce conditions.

Altalena Incident

Following the landing of the LST *Altalena* at Kfar Vitkin and Tel Aviv, where its arrival resulted in a fight between Hagana and Irgun on June 22, Bernadotte asked the Jewish authorities for an explanation of the incident and for information as to: (1) the number of people of military age who had landed; (2) the amount of munitions landed and what had been done with it; and (3) what measures the Jewish authorities had taken to prevent an infringement of the truce.

Full answers to all these questions are still awaited, but Shertok has given the following information in reply to a letter from the United Nations representative in Tel Aviv:

1. The Jewish authorities took all possible measures to prevent the landing of munitions, which they regarded as the principal threat to the truce.
2. The Irgun refused to obey the authority of the provisional government and gathered a force of four hundred men. Consequently, the Israeli army authorities were compelled to marshal a comparable force, which they did on the morning of Monday, June 21. (Note: this was the day the *Altalena* appeared at Kfar Vitkin, near Nathanaya).
3. If any immigrants did land from the *Altalena* they must have done so and dispersed during the night because all of the men who were killed or captured in the fighting on Monday were local members of Irgun.
4. In the course of the fighting, six IZL men were killed and eighteen wounded. Two were killed and six wounded in the Israeli army.
5. When the Irgun forces at Kfar Vitkin surrendered on Tuesday morning, they were only in possession of their personal arms. It was thus proved that the unloading of the arms and other war materials from the ship had not yet started, and the provisional government was satisfied that the whole quantity of such arms and war materials were actually consumed by flames when the *Altalena* took fire off Tel Aviv.
6. Two vessels of the Israeli coastal patrol proceeded to Kfar Vitkin during the night and when the *Altalena* tried to escape tracked her to Tel Aviv.

7. On Tuesday, units of IZL were rushed to the shore in Tel Aviv and occupied a few buildings near the beach. They tried to establish contact with the ship. As it was feared that this might result in an attempt to unload the arms by force, a warning had been issued and not heard, fire was opened on the *Altalena*, and the ship went up in flames. Many IZL men aboard and ashore were killed and wounded.

The story supplied to Bernadotte by UN observers is as follows:

1. On the morning of Monday, June 21, a United Nations aerial observer spotted a ship flying the Panamanian flag offshore near Nathanya. At this time, it appeared to be unloading boxes resembling ammunition cases.
2. Two United Nations ground observers were immediately ordered to the scene.
3. A Jewish colonel informed Bonde that a boat had appeared and he offered to escort UN observers to the scene, but he was told that observers had already been sent.
4. At 1:00 P.M. on the same day, Bonde himself went by plane to the scene. About six miles south of Nathanya, he saw about twenty men marching south. Offshore at Kfar Vitkin, he observed a black LST with its bow doors open and a barge running between the pier and the ship.

   Close to the piers he saw trucks loading cases that resembled ammunition cases or rifle cases. About two hundred men in khaki were around the pier. He also saw cases being carried in nearby fields and being covered with straw in an orchard. Bonde was unable to find a landing ground.
5. At 9:00 P.M. of the same day, another plane was sent to the same spot and observed loading still proceeding. The plane was fired at from the shore.

6. On the evening of Monday, June 21, Bonde was informed that United Nations observers had been prevented from reaching the ship by road guards who had stated that they were members of Irgun.
7. UN representatives at Tel Aviv immediately protested to Shertok (Moshe Sharrett) who stated at about 5:30 P.M. that he would arrange with the Israeli army authorities for observers to proceed to the scene.
8. At 8:30, the UN representatives were visited by a colonel who stated that UN observers could not be permitted on the scene of operations because they could not be allowed to see combat techniques of the Jewish army and its equipment.
9. The Jewish colonel was told that if observers were refused access to the scene they could not report properly on the situations.
10. At 5:00 A.M. on Tuesday, June 22, both ground and aerial observers were sent to Kfar Vitkin, accompanied by a Jewish liaison officer. They found that the LST had departed.
11. UN observers at Tel Aviv reported that at about midnight on June 21/22 an LST was seen approaching the coast off Tel Aviv, followed by two patrol vessels that exchanged fire with the ship. The ship ran aground just off the Kaeta Dan Hotel, headquarters of the United Nations observers at Tel Aviv.
12. At 11:00 A.M. on Tuesday, thirty men landed from the LST and ran into the town. Firing then started between Irgun and Hagana.
13. Unloading was attempted with a small landing craft but it had to return to the LST because of heavy fire from the shore.
14. About 4:00 P.M. fire from the shore (mortar or bazooka fire) set the LST afire. Some forty men were observed jumping into the water and swimming towards the shore. United Nations observers were withdrawn from the Kaeta Dan Hotel

because of the heavy fire and were not able to see what became of the swimmers.

Further Release at 2:30 P.M. Rhodes Time

Supplementing the report to the Security Council released in paraphrase earlier (above) the mediator filed a supplementary report containing the replies of the Israeli government (Shertok) to the questions raised by Bonde with regard to the *Altalena* incident:

1. Number of persons who landed from the *Altalena* and their whereabouts.

The Israeli government stated that published "boasts" of Irgun spokesmen placed the number of persons landed at eight hundred, but stated that the Israeli government is not in a position to ascertain the accuracy of this or any other figure. Nor do they have any information as to the whereabouts of such persons other than those in hospital.

2. Number of wounded and their whereabouts.

The Israeli government reported that at the time of writing (30 June) there were nineteen wounded members of the *Altalena* crew in the municipal hospital of Tel Aviv and two in the Beilinson Hospital of Kupat Holim. Thirty-seven men treated in the Tel Aviv hospital and eleven in the hospital of Kupat Holim have been released, their names being on record. Fourteen dead were among those brought to the Tel Aviv hospital following the battle on June 22.

3. Quantity of war material unloaded from the *Altalena*.

The Israeli government stated that, as already reported, it was satisfied that no war materials had been unloaded at Kfar Vitkin and that the whole cargo of the *Altalena* was consumed by fire.

> 4. Does the Israeli government still refuse to let the UN take care of the men and war materials landed?
>
> The Israeli government stated that in light of the foregoing, the question does not arise. Shertok reiterated a request for a conference with the mediator's chief of staff to determine as "precisely as possible" the rules of procedure to be observed regarding the access of UN observers to military positions or scenes of military action.

Thus it kept on, with either side sometimes stalling, sometimes bowing to the will of the United Nations as represented by Bernadotte. Certainly from the beginning it appeared that the truce supervision team had a well-nigh impossible job. Yet these teams exercised their authority as justly as they could, but they were often outwitted or left with inconclusive statements that contributed nothing towards the clarification of the situation.

Thus it was with the *Altalena* incident, when the Israeli government did not produce any convincing answer to the United Nations questions, and the matter was left unsettled—as were many others.

On July 4, we were given the text of Bernadotte's suggestions that had been sent to both Arabs and Jews around the twentieth of June. This was the result of his planning and his discussion with Arab and Zionist experts and the honest judgement of an honest man under difficult circumstances.

XVI
Introductory Statement

1. The resolution of the General Assembly of 14 May 1948 provides interalia that the United Nations mediator is to use his good offices to "promote a peaceful adjustment of the future situation of Palestine".

2. It follows that my prime objective as Mediator is to determine, on the basis of the fullest exploration, whether there is any possibility of reconciling, by peaceful means, the divergent and conflicting views and positions of the two sides.

3. The co-operative attitude manifested this far by both sides had made the truce possible which began on 11 June. This truce has brought a calmer atmosphere, more favorable to the task of mediation entrusted to me by the General Assembly. In this improved atmosphere I have talked with the representatives of both sides and have obtained a very clear impression of their positions on the question of the future of Palestine. I have also profited from the information afforded by the technical consultant whom each side has designated in response to my request.

4. The basic issues arising from the positions taken by the opposing parties relate to partition, the establishment of a Jewish State, and Jewish immigration.

5. I have thoroughly studied, weighed and appraised the positions taken by the two parties. I interpret my role as Mediator not as one involving the handing down of decisions on the future situation of Palestine, but as one of offering suggestions on the

basis of which further discussions might take place and possibly counter-suggestions be put forth looking towards a peaceful settlement of this difficult problem. My suggestions at this state, then, must clearly be of such a nature as to provide a reasonable framework of reference within which the two parties may find it possible to continue their consultations towards the end of a peaceful adjustment.

6. My analysis has taken into account the equities involved, and the aspirations, fears and motivations of the parties. It has also taken account of the realities of the existing situation. *It has convinced me that on grounds of equity as on practical grounds, it is impossible for me as Mediator to call upon either party to surrender completely its position.* On the light of this analysis I see a possibility of an adjustment which would give adequate reassurances to both parties as regards the vital factors in their respective positions. But the realisation of this possibility depends upon the willingness of the parties to explore all avenues for a peaceful adjustment and their readiness not to resume armed conflict as a means of settling their differences.

7. Despite the present conflict, there is a common denominator in Palestine which, happily, is acceptable to and affirmed by both sides. *This is the recognition of the necessity for peaceful relations between Arabs and Jews in Palestine and of the principle of economic unity.*

8. It is with this common denominator especially in mind that I put forth the accompanying suggestions in outline as a basis for discussion. The suggestions, I must emphasize, are submitted with no intimation of preciseness or finality. They are designed solely to explore the possible bases for further discussions and mediation, and to elicit from the parties their reactions and further views. Moreover, any plans which might result from these suggestions could be workable only if voluntarily accepted and applied. *There can be no question of their imposition.*

9. I should make perfectly clear my intentions as regards future procedure. If it develops that the suggestions herewith presented, or other suggestions subsequently presented which may arise from reactions to those now put forth, provide a basis for discussion, I will carry on with the discussions as long as may prove necessary and fruitful. If however, these or subsequent suggestions, if any should emerge, are rejected as a basis for discussion, which I earnestly hope will not occur, I shall promptly report the circumstances fully to the Security Council and shall feel free to submit such conclusions to the Security Council as I may consider appropriate.

Count Folke Bernadotte
United Nations Mediator on Palestine
Rhodes, 27 June 1948

XVII

Suggestions Presented by the Mediator on Palestine

The Mediator advances the following suggestions as a possible basis for discussion.

1. That, subject to the willingness of the directly interested parties to consider such an arrangement, Palestine, as defined in the original Mandate entrusted to the United Kingdom in 1922, that is, including Transjordan, might form a Union comprising two Members: one Arab and one Jewish.

2. That the boundaries of the two Members are determined in the first instance by negotiation with the assistance of the Mediator and on the basis of suggestions to be made by him. When agreement is reached on the main outlines of the boundaries, they will be definitely fixed by a boundaries commission.

3. That the purposes and functions of the Union should be to promote common economic interests, to operate and maintain common service, including customs and excise, to undertake development projects, and to coordinate foreign policy and measures for common defence.

4. That the functions and authority of the Union might be exercised through a Central Council and such other organs as the Members of the Union may determine.

5. That, subject to the provisions of the instrument of Unions, each member of the Union may exercise full control over its own affairs, including its foreign relations.

6. That immigration within its own borders should be within the competence of each Member, provided that following a period of two years from the establishment of the Union, either Member would be entitled to request the Council of the Union to review the immigration policy of the other Member and to render a ruling thereon in terms of the common interests of the Union. In the event of the inability of the Council to reach a decision on the matter, the issue could be referred by either Member to the Economic and Social Council of the United Nations, whose decision, taking into account the principle of economic absorptive capacity, would be binding on the Member whose policy is at issue.

7. That religious and minority rights be fully protected by each Member of the Union and guaranteed by the United Nations.

8. That Holy Places, religious buildings and sites be preserved, and that existing rights in respect of the same be fully guaranteed by each Member of the Union.

9. That recognition be accorded to the right of residents of Palestine who, because of conditions created by the conflict there, have left their normal places of abode, to return to their homes without restriction and to regain possession of their property.

Count Folke Bernadotte
United Nations Mediator on Palestine
Rhodes, 27 June 1948

Release Time:1800 GMT, Sunday, 4 July 1948

XVIII

Annex to the Suggestions: Territorial Matters

With regards to paragraph 2 of the Suggestions, it is considered that certain territorial arrangements might be worthy of consideration. These might be along the following lines:

1. Inclusion of the whole or part of the Negev in Arab territory.
2. Inclusion of the whole or part of Western Galilee in Jewish territory.
3. Inclusion of the City of Jerusalem in Arab territory, with municipal autonomy for the Jewish community and special arrangements for the protection of the Holy Places.
4. Consideration of the status of Jaffa.
5. Establishment of a free port at Haifa, the area of the free port to include the refineries and terminals.
6. Establishment of a free airport at Lydda.

Count Folke Bernadotte
United Nations Mediator on Palestine
Rhodes, 27 June 1948 Release

Time: 1800 GMT, Sunday, 4 July 1948

Count Bernadotte seriously believed he had provided the Jews and Arabs with the only possible basis for a peaceful solution of the Palestine problem and injected a veiled threat that if they did not accept these or other suggestions arising out of further discussion, he would take the matter to the Security Council.

He made it clear that he was proposing a solution both on the ground of equity and reality. He did not try to pass judgement of whether Jew or Arab was right or wrong, but went on the premise that both were in the Holy Land, and both had seized various parts of the country and that possession was nine-tenths of the law. Right or wrong, this was his plan.

The Arab League invited him to Cairo to discuss the matter with leaders of all the Arab world. He returned on July 4 from there but would not tell correspondents whether his scheme had been accepted or rejected. He merely announced he had the Arabs' reply and was going on to Tel Aviv to see the Jews and then back to Cairo.

''We have done our best despite the extreme difficulty of finding something which others had not proposed previously. Don't think we believe this plan marvellous, but it is the best effort we have made. We believe we have tried our best,'' said Bernadotte to reporters on Rhodes. He looked very weary.

His proposals were very courageous. He gave Galilee to the Jews and the Negev to the Arabs. He said internationalization would not work.

''Look at Berlin,'' he told me, ''it doesn't work. The plan to internationalize Jerusalem might have worked for some time and then broken down. Anyway, Jerusalem lies within Arab territory.'' The mediator also realised that several Arab nations would not favor the idea of the Arab part of Palestine being linked to Transjordan.

But on the whole he had given his honest opinion, taking into consideration the facts at his disposal and the advice of his aides. As it turned out, the advice was not very good.

Time was running short and only a few days were left before the truce ended and the two sides grappled with each other again. Yet the two had not had enough time to fully consider Bernadotte's plan and suggest any counterproposals. So he made two new proposals to the Jews and Arabs. He suggested that the truce be prolonged and that in any case, whether they accepted to prolong the ceasefire or not, they should demilitarize Jerusalem and possibly Haifa. The demilitarized zones would be placed under United Nations guards recruited from the United States, France, and Belgium.

By that time we got the news at Rhodes that the Arabs had decided to reject the proposals to prolong the truce and had rejected Bernadotte's plan, as had the Israelis. Thus the war was due to start again. We were gloomy on the island. It meant going back to the deadly race in Amman, driving madly to the frontlines and back again over dangerous roads to file our stories from the Transjordanian capital. It meant sweating under the blazing sun as we went back and forth across the Dead Sea valley, three hundred feet under sea level, and absolute hell during the daytime.

Our gloom had deepened by a report that a French United Nations observer had died in Palestine when his jeep blew up on a mine. Commandant René Labarrière was killed and another Frenchman wounded. On July 8, I wrote: "The faded blue flag of the United Nations is flying at half-mast over Bernadotte's headquarters today. It is mourning the death of a United Nations observer, but it also symbolizes the demise of peace efforts and mourning for the war which will start again. As the flag's blueness faded in the torrid Aegean sun, so hopes of settlement were fading in the heat of conference rooms in Cairo and Tel Aviv."

Bernadotte felt that it was the Egyptians who had forced the other Arabs to reject the United Nations proposals. He believed that the other Arab nations, and particularly Transjordan, would have accepted the Bernadotte plan. Commenting on his mission, he said, "I don't think I am a broken man, or that I feel I have failed in my mission. I am happy to notice that both sides have said they hoped I would come back and talk to them again. If they want to use me again, I am at their disposal—providing the Security Council approves.

"We have achieved some results by the truce. Tomorrow the war is on again. If one of the parties will have victories, it will be in a better position to negotiate. Similarly, the party suffering military setbacks will be in a worse position. The losers may then want to reconsider my suggestions, but I think that then it will be too late to discuss these suggestions. Both sides are taking terrible risks. I am not the loser, but I am one hundred percent sure that both parties will lose.

"War never pays. That has been my experience and yours."

Although Bernadotte's voice was as firm as the monocle screwed into his eye, there was no doubt that he was disappointed. The Arabs had rejected his plan because they felt it gave the Jews too much, and the Jews had refused to limit their immigration, wanted a straight partition and no union, and claimed Jerusalem as a Jewish city.

Both sides bluntly told Bernadotte that they did not even consider his suggestions formed the basis for discussion. A resumption of hostilities seemed inevitable, and the mediator concentrated on trying to save Jerusalem from further destruction.

"I do not consider that my mission is at an end as a result of this temporary setback. I will continue to work on the task assigned to me by the May 14 resolution of the United Nations General Assembly with a view to attaining at the earliest possible day a peaceful adjustment for the future situation of Palestine," barked Bernadotte in his precise but clipped English.

The mediator told press reporters in Rhodes that the Jews had accepted to prolong the thirty-day truce due to end on July 9 on the same conditions as governed the original ceasefire, but the Arabs had refused. They said that their experiences during the past four weeks did not justify their accepting. They claimed that the United Nations had been powerless to prevent the steady stream of arms the Jews had been bringing into the Holy Land and that the United Nations had not been able to use any force in coping with violations of the truce agreement.

During all these critical days, Bernadotte kept flying back and forth between Cairo, Tel Aviv, and Rhodes.

On July 9, the day the war was to restart, Bernadotte took off at dawn with Bunche and other assistants. His white painted United Nations plane carried him to an undisclosed destination and no amount of persuasion could reveal where he was going. That night we saw him returning, and he asked us to come to his suite where he announced he had been to Amman and Haifa and had sent "urgent appeals" to both Jews and Arabs for a ten-day unconditional ceasefire while he went to Lake Success to discuss the entire matter with the United Nations.

"The purpose of my trip will be to resume my mediation efforts in the interests of peace and the peoples of Palestine, both Arabs and Jews alike, and the grave concern felt for the preservation of Jerusalem," said Bernadotte.

In Amman, Bernadotte had met King Abdullah and discussed the demilitarization of Jerusalem and "other things." The shooting had restarted in the Holy Land but on a limited scale. From Haifa he sent his appeal to the Jewish government, and he stopped over at Beirut to radio his appeal to the leaders of all the Arab nations.

The situation was growing more tense. Some serious fighting had developed in which the Jews made some substantial gains especially on the Egyptian-held front. The Security Council ordered a new truce on July 15. Bernadotte returned to Rhodes and within a week of the new truce had swung into action. He began assigning American, French, and Belgian military observers to Palestine and neighboring areas.

First he brought them to Rhodes where they were briefed before going over. He told his observers that the truce would continue until a peaceful adjustment of Palestine was reached. In a large hall at the Hotel des Roses, he told the first wave of observers, "You are all VIPs on this mission." The Americans included army, navy and marine corps officers. The United States government placed three destroyers and the French one corvette at the disposal of the mediator for coastal observation.

The observers had to be objective and exercise a considerable amount of tact. But the weakness, right from the start, was that they were powerless to enforce any action. Should fighting break out, all they could do was to report the matter objectively and use any moral force at their disposal. As it turned out, moral force was not enough to cope with many of the situations that arose. Already that lesson had been learnt during the ten-day fighting between the two truces when the Israelis had won considerable ground on several fronts, especially against the Arab forces in Northern Palestine and against the Transjordan army which withdrew from the vital, strategic Lydda-Ramleh area.

The United Nations mediation and observers found in late July 1948 that the attitude of the Jewish political leaders had toughened since these military victories between the two truces. The Arabs in the meantime continued to refuse to recognize the presence of a Jewish state.

Despite this deadlock, both sides welcomed the ceasefire, the Jews because they had gained control of almost all they wanted at the time, and the Arabs because they were very short of supplies. Both sides also feared that a further defiance of the United Nations would result in sanctions against the guilty side.

But as the second truce began, it was obvious that the Jews' policy had changed. They now said they were entitled to more territory in any final settlement than they had previously asked for because they had managed to gain control of more land during the ten-day fighting. They claimed the war had been restarted by the Arabs. They hinted they would demand both Galilee and the Negev in Southern Palestine. The United Nations partition plan gave the Jews the Negev and Galilee to the Arabs. Count Bernadotte's suggestions reversed this, with the Negev going to the Arabs and Galilee to the Jews, simply because this was already a fait accompli.

The Jews then alleged that had the fighting continued, they would have driven the Egyptians back in Southern Palestine and "liberated" the Negev. They also pointed out that they had made substantial gains including the capture of Nazareth in Galilee.

As both sides jockeyed for new positions, the Arabs countered by saying that all Jewish gains had been made because the Jews smuggled in supplies during the truce period and because a world blockade against the Arabs prevented them from obtaining supplies, especially from Britain who had "betrayed" the Arabs.

There seemed to be little doubt that the Israelis managed to get a steady stream of supplies, including Flying Fortresses and artillery. The airlift into Israel was well organised from both sides of the Iron Curtain.

The Arabs had no such assistance, so they were merely content to claim that had they been able to bring in supplies and had they been free of United Nations pressure, they would have continued to advance on all fronts. But they claimed "British treachery" had placed them at a disadvantage. The Arabs charged that the British officers in Transjordan's Arab Legion had ordered the unnecessary withdrawal from the vital Lydda-Ramleh area upon orders from the British government as further pressure to oblige the Arabs to accept the United Nations cease-fire order.

There were several disagreements in the Arab camp. The Transjordanians blamed the Egyptians; the Syrians, the Lebanese; the Lebanese, the Palestinians; and so on. Each accused the other of treachery. All agreed that the British, and indeed the entire outside world, had conspired against the Arabs. Bitterly they pointed out that for once Russia and the United States seemed to agree to block the Arabs. In short, the Arabs blamed everybody but themselves.

On Rhodes, more and more UN observers were arriving. Mature French, Belgian, and American officers came in, got briefed, and were went to their various posts in Palestine or the neighboring areas. General Aage Lundstroom and nine Swedish officers arrived to become Bernadotte's chief of staff, and his officers were to undertake special assignments for Bernadotte.

With all these observers, the new communications system set up by Gen. Frank Stoner, the UN's chief communication officer, and the streamlined organisation, it was still very difficult often to fully check skirmishes, raids, and manoeuvres carried out. Both Arabs and Jews would send exaggerated complaints, with only a basis of truth, and at other times they were unfounded reports.

The cable sent by Bernadotte to Trygvie Lie indicates the type of problems the observers were up against, and their relative helplessness to do anything about it. This cable was sent on July 30, 1948:

> Text of a report forwarded by the Mediator today to the Secretary General of the United Nations for transmission to the President of the Security Council, Lake Success:
>
> First complaints received Rhodes from either side against alleged violations of truce beginning 18 July were communicated to you by my telegrams m141 and m146 stop Have since received new complaints including copies those addressed directly Lake Success by Syrian Foreign Minister para.
>
> Arrival first contingents observers on the spot has permitted me to start both investigations and settlement of local incidents para.
>
> 1. Conditions on Syrian front particularly in Banias region from 19 to 22 July had given rise to complaints and counter complaints including protests by Syria against air raids stop U.N.

observers reported on 25th July there had been no incident on that front for last 48 hours.

2. Following serious situation which arose south Haifa has now apparently calmed down owing prompt action U.N. observers stop On 22 July complaint against the attack since 20 July of Arab villages Jaba, Ein Ghazal and Ijzim, South of Haifa was handed to Mediator's representatives in Beirut stop

On 23 July he received new complaint concerning aerial bombing same villages on 21 and 22 July stop same complaint with request for inquiry was received by Mediator 24th July from Secretary General Arab League who had been informed of alleged air attacks by Iraqi Commander in Amman stop

On 25th July U.N. observers attacked Iraqui HQ Nablus reported complaint of attacks against three villages adding were occupied by Arab irregulars supported by Iraqui army which threatened retaliatory air raids unless attacks ceased immediately stop U.N. observers informed Jewish authorities of above threat stop On 27 July following telegram was received from Mediator's representative Beirut quote Secretary General Arab League notified personally serious incidents Jewish attacks Jaba, Ein Ghazal, Ijzim four thousand refugees and tens of thousand captured and massacred urgent action required or Arab section follows unquote

Investigation was immediately ordered and following report was received 28 July from Mediator's acting chief of staff Haifa quote reference request made by Mediator that investigation be made of reports by Secretary General Arab League regarding actions taken against Arabs in the villages of Ein Ghazal, Jaba, Ijzim, observer party consisting of seven U.N. officer observers were dispatched to investigate on the morning of 28th July stop As result of this inspection no evidence was found to support claims of massacres and capture stop following evidence was found:

1. All three villages are deserted except for one woman who appeared to be insane stop

2. In village of Jaba four small stone buildings were wholly or partially destroyed as result of explosion of small aerial bombs artillery or mortar stop

3. Two bodies found in Ein Ghazal stop Body of women appeared to have been killed by an explosion stop Other body of man apparently killed by a gun shot stop Bodies appeared to have been dead for about ten days stop

4. Jewish liaison officers admitted that four Arabs in village of Jaba are prisoners and nine in village of Ein Ghazal had been killed during a subquote police unsubquote raid three days ago stop will make more definite report later unquote para.:

THREE: Situation Jerusalem 26 July reported by Mediator's representative as follows no action by regular troops action by irregulars continues with sniping on small scale para.:

FOUR: U.N. representative Jerusalem reported first Jerusalem convoy since truce renewed was turned back at Latrun 29 July by Arab soldiers and civilians stop Matter being investigated and taken up with Arab authorities para.

FIVE: Note Egyptian Prime Minister received 30 July alleges two landing craft loaded ammunition and war material left Bari Italy 26 July for Palestine stop Acting chief of staff instructed take necessary measures involving observers land sea and air report called attention Tel Aviv para.

Other incidents brought my notice by governments similarly investigated and as far as possible settled on spot stop

Count Folke Bernadotte

Other cables sent by Bernadotte complained to the United Nations because they were not sending him all he needed quickly. He told the UN that they were slow in moving and openly said his cables were "very frank." He could not cope with the complaints coming in from Jews and Arabs because he still lacked the required number of observers and transport.

Out of fifteen C-47 planes he had requested, only four had arrived, and none of eight Beechcrafts. He had requested helicopters and one hundred and fifty jeeps. Only thirty jeeps had come by July 31. Some official in the United Nations, who obviously did not know even then that the Israelis still refused to allow any British subjects into their state, had sent five five-seater Consols manned by British crews. Bernadotte was only able to use them outside Palestine on ferry flights. To make matters worse, the Greek cable employees went on strike before the United Nations communications were quite ready.

Bernadotte decided to send Ralph Bunche to Lake Success to tell the people there what it was like trying to prevent a war in the Middle East without getting any real help from the U.N. He himself decided to make one final five-day swing through the area to convince Jews and Arabs to demilitarize Jerusalem. Then he was flying to Sweden to preside over the International Red Cross meeting. Even there he was planning to put in a plea for the hundreds of thousands of Palestine Arab refugees who were now living in filth in the neighboring Arab states.

With Bernadotte on the swing was Australian Sir Raphael Cilentor, refugee director in the UN Social Affairs Department. The mediator had realized that the Arabs were very bitter over the entire Palestine conflict and felt that the outside world had unfairly sided with the Jews against them. He hoped to gain some of their confidence in trying to make life easier for the refugees.

During his visit to various cities, Bernadotte found a tense situation, with considerable sniping in Jerusalem and reports of heavy firing between the Israelis and Egyptians in the Negev. He also found the state of the refugees terrible.

Bernadotte then made one more visit to Jerusalem before leaving for Sweden and again tried to get Jews and Arabs to accept his demilitarization proposals. He found the Arabs ready, but the Jews were not in favor of demilitarization as the best solution for peace. They believed that if they were given Jerusalem, they could quickly restore peace. There was considerable firing in the Holy City, not just rifles, but mortars and light artillery.

Reports received by Bernadotte and transmitted to the press said that the UN observers, sent to indicate who was starting the firing, blamed the Jews. ''The mischief for the shooting in

Jerusalem is from the Jewish side,'' said Bernadotte. He said his observers went out during the night and reported that the Jews were provoking the clashes.

When he left for Sweden on August 12, the problem of Palestine was still undecided. He took some of his staff with him and a couple of correspondents. I was one of them. From the Land of the Midnight Sun, we continued to watch the troubles in the Holy Land.

XIX
Assassinations and Upheavals

The month I spent in Stockholm with Count Bernadotte was a wonderful change from the tension of the Middle East. For years, we all had been living in the throes of one explosion after the other. A few hours by plane and we were among peace-loving people who seemed to have no troubles or worries. To me, the absence of policemen in the streets was very noticeable. For years, I had seen steel-helmeted police, armed civilians, and belligerent forces. For one month I wandered pleasantly among the hospitable Swedes, listened to Bernadotte and others at the International Red Cross, and watched the delegates from all over the world talk in quiet, subdued voices.

There were princes and princesses from the small states of Europe, dynamic delegations from the United States and Britain, uniformed representatives from Latin America. Some were genuinely concerned with the humanitarian duties of the conference; for others it was a pleasant holiday, and for some, it was a political platform.

But during that month my admiration of Bernadotte grew steadily. There was seldom a day that we did not sit for some time together and go over the developments in Palestine. There was so much the man wanted to do, so many shortcomings of which he was conscious, and despite all obstacles, he maintained a cheerful opinion that in the end some justice would be achieved.

It was with a feeling of sadness that Bernadotte found it necessary to propose a solution for Palestine in which justice would have to be tempered with reality. But because of his desire to reach a settlement that might restore peace to a troubled land and to end the misery of masses who had never wanted this conflict, he worked to reach a practical solution and sought to get the United Nations to impose such a plan regardless of the objections of the local politicians.

I often wondered what would induce a man like Bernadotte to leave the peace and security of a beautiful home in Sweden, the affection of his family, and the already responsible tasks he had in his homeland to go to the Middle East on a mission that had scared away many before him. Certainly the challenge of the task appealed to him and aroused all his humanitarian instincts. He was not the man to refuse to help suffering people.

There were some, who either willfully or misguidedly, accused Bernadotte of being a British agent, the stooge of the Jews, or the puppet of the Arabs. Among his accusers were men who were supposed to be of an intellectual caliber and social position that should have taught them better.

Bernadotte was convinced that the Arabs had every right to be in Palestine. He thought that the Zionists were wrong in the way they had tried to conquer the land and drive tens of thousands of Arabs into refugee camps. Yet he considered that for the Jews the excuse of years of persecution had driven them to an act of desperation. On the whole he was not concerned with what started the war. He wanted to end it. The fact he had to face was that both the Jews and the Arabs were in Palestine. He tried to divide the land, but the Arabs refused to recognize that any part of the land should go to the Jews, and the Israelis wanted more land than he was willing to grant them.

So once more we boarded the white-painted United Nations plane from Bromma airport to return to the Middle East. As the plane took off, I took one last look at Stockholm and the islands, then closed my eyes to sleep. Bernadotte was looking down on his city. A few minutes later a pillow landed on my head, and I saw the grinning face of the mediator down the aisle. He beckoned to me, and when I had gone over to his side, he said, "You'll have the time to sleep later. Now you must look on some of the beautiful scenery below. We are diverting slightly from our course to fly over my father's castle."

Soon we were there, and the plane flew low over the beautiful estate. On one of the balconies a tiny figure waved a handkerchief.

"That's my father," Bernadotte said quietly, and although he knew the man could not see him, his hand moved across the porthole. The plane flew over the castle again and dipped to salute Prince Oscar.

"He is a very old man," said Bernadotte, "I may not see him again."

Little did he think that within a few days he would be dead and that his sorrowing father would outlive him.

Rhodes was the same. Bernadotte and Bunche immediately went to work and then decided on a quick swing through the area before going to Paris where the United Nations were gathering at the Palais de Chaillot.

From Beirut I headed for Egypt where I was planning to cover the mediator's meetings with the Arab League then gathered in Alexandria. After the Alexandria meeting, Bernadotte went off to Jerusalem. There a Jewish terrorist shot and killed him in a well-organized holdup.

The United Nations mourned his death. He was flown to Stockholm and buried with all the honors he deserved. The United Nations met, condemned the brutal Israeli act, and quickly forgot about it.

The war resumed in Palestine, particularly in the south between the Egyptian and Israeli forces. Not only did the war resume but never had it been so intense and deadly as at that moment. Strong Israeli forces pushed back the badly equipped Egyptians almost completely out of Palestine. An Egyptian force was besieged and held out in Falouga. Bitter fighting took place even inside Egypt where a Jewish column had penetrated to try to cut off the large Egyptian force at Gaza.

The United Nations told acting mediator Ralph Bunche to take over and get an armistice signed. On January 11, 1949, Bunche and his team, almost the same as the one that had worked under Bernadotte, landed on Rhodes. From the start this time, Israeli and Egyptian armistice delegations were present. From January 12 to February 24, Bunche and General Riley, chief of the United Nations observers, spent hours in delicate, nerve-wracking negotiations with Jews and Egyptians.

Both sides wrangled, bluffed, debated interpretations of words, phrases, and intentions. At times, the deadlocks seemed insurmountable. But Bunche, with apparently greater patience than Job and a capacity for hard work such as few men have, managed to keep the talks going.

I got to Rhodes on January 15 and reestablished contact with my old friends. I also saw many faces I had not seen for a long time. They were those of the Israeli delegations, including Gen. Yigal Yadin, then assistant chief of staff and later chief of staff of the Israeli army.

It was bitterly cold on Rhodes and not as pleasant as the summer days when we had been there with Bernadotte. The rain kept us cooped up in the hotel. Anyway there was no place we could go. For the press, the armistice negotiations were very frustrating. Both sides had promised not to give out any information and left that to the UN's information officer. There was very little solid news, although occasionally an item slipped out often deliberately.

On January 17, I went to Bunche's room to have a chat with him. Quite a group was gathered there. They were United Nations officials, gathered from many countries. They included American Marine General Riley, Frenchman Henri Vigier, John Reedman, a South African, Constantine Stavropoulos, legal expert from Greece, and Doreen Daughton, Bunche's secretary.

Bunche seemed to think that things were progressing satisfactorily and hoped to be able to get a concrete result in the armistice talks between the Egyptians and Jews quite shortly.

The conversation then shifted to a lengthy debate on where the past mediation had failed and the various factors involved. Bunche started off by admitting that "in this very room" he and his men had led Bernadotte up the garden path by strongly advising that he should concentrate on Transjordan to bring about the truce. Bunche said they should have known that this country, so much under British influence, would only do what Britain wanted. Right from the start, they should have known that Egypt was the only country that they should deal with. "It can stand against Britain and has done so." By negotiating mainly with Egypt, the UN team might have spared itself and all concerned many difficulties, said Bunche.

Reedman was not of this opinion. He felt that it was only the latest developments that had brought the situation around to enable Egypt to be the chosen nation to deal with. He believed that before the Egyptians could not have been of any use. It was only after the various developments that things had made it possible to work with them. He was convinced that in the beginning Egypt did not feel the need to negotiate.

Bunche opposed this thesis, saying he felt that the United Nations mediation should have put off the first truce. This would have ultimately facilitated the mediation. Had the fighting gone on a little longer at the beginning, there would have been less fighting later, he contended. While both sides had been willing to sign the first truce, there were definite indications that a quick truce would only mean difficult mediation later.

"If we had given them another month of fighting, one of the two sides would have come running up to ask for mediation, and then it would have been effective," said Bunche.

Reedman replied he did not believe that Israelis would have come running up to ask for mediation because they had already started building the ''Burma road'' from Tel Aviv to Jerusalem and had almost finished it by the time the first truce came about. The road skirted the Arab-held positions barring the route of Jerusalem, and the Jews would have been able to send a steady stream of supplies to their people in the Holy City.

To this Bunche retorted that it would not have been easy to keep all Jerusalem fed and that the Jews were in a very difficult position.

Reedman answered that, even before the first truce, ships had started bringing in arms and equipment for the Jews and that their position would have been far better if the truce had not come. Another month's fighting would have seen them gaining the upper hand. He also remarked that Arab disunity, evident right from the start, was another major factor in allowing the Jews to improve their position.

''Even before the truce, positions were static, and the Arabs were not gaining much ground simply because they had no coordinated plan of attack,'' Reedman said.

General Riley then came into the conversation and said that, as a military man, he felt that the Arabs had the upper hand although they made a series of stupid blunders. He blamed King Abdullah for attacking Jerusalem and not going straight for the Tel Aviv sector and the Iraqis for the independent action in the Beisan area rather than striking for Qalqilya to cut the Tel Aviv-Haifa road. He admitted that the Iraqis later revised their plan but it was too late, and when the truce came, the Jews were able to prepare much faster than the Arabs.

''If I had been the supreme commander of the Arab forces during the first month of fighting, I would have swept the Jews into the sea. The Arabs had superior equipment to the Jews, and they held excellent positions. The Egyptians had advanced very close to Tel Aviv, and the Iraqis could have cut the Tel Aviv-Haifa road.''

Then the great debate started on what were British intentions. What was their policy, and why their various paradoxical actions? Bunche asked me whether I had heard any report of oil in the Negev. Reedman, the UN's economic expert on Palestine, said that all reports he had seen indicated that there was little oil in the Negev as compared to other areas and that what little drilling had been done was unproductive. I suggested that there might be other minerals and again Reedman said that reports were not very satisfactory.

Riley then said, ''What about uranium?'' and Reedman admitted that so far there had been no indication one way or the other.

Vigier and others present thought that there were strategic as well as economic considerations. They all felt it was no coincidence that while the British had made several attempts to partition Palestine, all their proposals had given the Negev to the Arabs but never to the Jews. Even the Peel report was willing to give the Arab-dominated Galilee area to the Jews, but not the sparsely populated Negev.

We sat sipping cocktails and talking in the comfortable rooms. Stavropoulos tried to concentrate on a story he had been reading in the *New Yorker* when he had started our conversation and seemed exasperated because he could not finish it, as he was too interested in the general discussion.

What struck me was that during the discussion there was never an admission that the UN had failed in its task, although they admitted they had made mistakes and tried to justify them. All of them admitted that arms were coming in under their very noses to Tel Aviv and Haifa and that the Zionists had completely disregarded the United Nations, fully conscious that it was powerless to clamp any sanctions. This failure to make Arab and Jew respect the rules contributed much to the chaotic situation.

Bunche was very anxious to reach an armistice between the Israelis and Egypt first, then the other Arab states, and then hand the Palestine problem to the Conciliation Commission. By February 24, he had succeeded in getting the first armistice signed. It was not foolproof, as became evident later. It paved the way for the subsequent armistice with Transjordan, which was signed on April 3. While negotiations were proceeding on Rhodes between the Israelis and the Transjordanians, the Jews and the Lebanese were meeting under the chairmanship of Henri Vigier at Ras Nakura, on the Lebanese-Palestinian frontier to reach armistices that were duly signed. Only Iraq refused to sign a formal armistice, but since it had no common frontier with Israel, it was not important.

The armistice agreements permitted many soldiers to return to their homes. Among those, the beleaguered Egyptian garrison at Falouja, which had refused to surrender to the Israelis, marched out proudly.

One of the battle-weary officers was a young major, Gamal Abdel Nasser. The Palestine campaign had exposed him to rot within the army and inside Egypt. As he marched out, his mind was already working on the plan that was ultimately to sweep away the complacency and corruption of the court at Cairo.

XX
Coup d'État in Syria

The Syrian negotiations, although ultimately signed, proved a little difficult. They were interrupted by some dramatic developments in the shape of an unexpected coup d'état.

There was not much doing on Rhodes as the two sides bickered about details, and no news filtered through the press. So when General Riley told Sam Brewer of the *New York Times* and myself that he intended leaving for Damascus in half an hour, and would be glad to take us along, we did not hesitate.

Our aim was to get a car to take us to Beirut where we could enjoy some decent food and meet some friends. Bad weather delayed our arrival in Damascus, and we decided to spend the night there, see what news might develop from the meetings between General Riley and Colonel Husni Zaim, the Syrian Army Chief of Staff, and then proceed to Beirut the following day.

Damascus was pretty dull. The people were still depressed by the developments in Palestine, and there was little or no entertainment. I went to see a few friends, sat in the Orient Palace talking to some of the local politicians; there was general bitterness at the turn of events. By midnight I was in bed and eager to get to Beirut the following day.

It was still dark when I heard the roar of motorcycles, armored cars, and the sound of unusual activity in the street. The rumbling increased as a strong force approached the hotel.

There were a series of orders and more noise as the troops took up positions. From my bed I thought it might be sentries being posted around the Orient Palace in case some Syrian or Palestinian, embittered by the Palestine affair, should try to assassinate General Riley.

The general had seen Colonel Zaim briefly that afternoon and was planning to see him again, as the Syrian had been very busy. I thought I might have to spend another day in Damascus and didn't like the idea. It was still very early, about four in the morning, and I decided to try and sleep again despite the noise. But the din continued. I poked my head out of the window and politely asked the soldiers below if they could be somewhat quieter to enable their guests to sleep.

A long-haired Syrian soldier, wearing the desert headdress and a very grimy uniform, looked up at me and muttered something I couldn't understand. I noticed that he and his comrades were not the soldiers normally stationed in the Syrian capital. I also noticed that there were machine gun nests at various points and some armored cars. They must be really worried about Riley, I thought.

As I started talking again, an officer appeared and said, "I'm sorry if we can't be quieter, but we feel that considering the coup d'état we've just carried out, we've been very quiet indeed."

Coup d'état! I threw on some clothes and dashed down the stairs. At the door another long-haired, wild-eyed Bedouin soldier from the desert tribes poked a gun under my nose, and I pulled up hurriedly.

"No one is allowed to leave here, and no one walks in the streets," he grunted. With the gun pointed straight at me, I raised no objection whatsoever. At that moment, a young captain whom I had met in Palestine, came up. He gave me the news. Col. Husni Zaim and some other officers had pulled off a bloodless coup d'état. President Shukri Kuwatly and Premier Jamil Mardam were under arrest, as were some others.

The army was in control. There was a curfew until further notice, unless you had a pass signed by Colonel Zaim. I phoned up army headquarters and cautiously asked for some of the officers I knew. Finally, I got somebody on the line and in a while an officer came bringing me a curfew pass. I hurried over to headquarters, which was a beehive of activity. Communiqués were being prepared, broadcasts explaining that the army had decided to rid Syria of its corrupt, decadent leaders. Could I send any cables? No. Could I phone? No. And I was warned that if anybody phoned me from Beirut or Amman, the wires would be tapped and it would be wise to talk carefully.

The new military junta included such people as Adib el Shishakly who had been in Palestine and whom I knew from there. There was also Colonel Sami el Hinnawi.

The frontiers were closed and no one was supposed to go in or out of Syria. But with activity concentrated in Damascus and the key towns of Aleppo, Homs, and Hama, the check on the frontiers was not airtight. I got through to Beirut where I sent the first eyewitness account of the first coup d'état in Syria.

Col. Husni Zaim became field marshal and president of the Syrian Republic and appointed Mohsen el Barazi as prime minister. He was a dynamic personality, with many virtues but quite a few faults. It was not long after that his former military comrades ganged up on him, and the second coup d'état was carried out. It was not bloodless. Zaim and Barazi were shot, and Colonel Sami el Hinnawi took over.

Then came Hinnawi's turn. Col. Adib Shishakly organized the third coup d'état, although he kept discreetly away from the public eyes. Officially his job was deputy chief of staff but he was generally recognized as the strongman. Hinnawi escaped to Lebanon where some relatives of Barazi's subsequently hunted him down and killed him.

Shishakly restored Parliament and placed eighty-year-old Hashem el Atassy as president, and a cabinet was formed. The minister of defence was an army colonel, and he controlled both the army and the police, previously controlled by the minister of interior.

When the politicians thought they were strong enough to defy the military clique, they created a crisis. Again Shishakly stepped in, threw out the ageing president and the cabinet that had just been formed, and once more established a military regime. He charged the politicians were corrupt and leading the country to ruin. As new president was Col. Fawzi Selo, and Shishakly came into the open as chief of staff and the avowed strongman of Syria.

Shishakly later became the undisputed strongman of Syria and ruled his country virtually single-handed until January 1954 when another military coup d'état overthrew him.

Once more, the government was handed over to the civilians, and elections brought back the exiled Shukry el Kuwatly as president of Syria. Ever since Husni Zaim had expelled him, Kuwatly had lived in Egypt. Now, several years and many ulcers older, he returned. Another politician, Khaled el Azm, was defeated in the presidential elections.

Cabinets succeeded each other during the coming years, but one obvious development was the fast-growing power of the leftist Baath Socialist party, led by Akram el Hourani. The small, beak-nosed Hourani befriended many of the younger officers in the army. Hourani had a political program that appealed to many of the younger men, who hoped for a better future for their country. Among his most stalwart supporters, Hourani had two ambitious young officers, Col. Adnan el Malki, deputy chief of staff and Maj. (later Lt. Col.) Abdel Hamid Serraj, who became the head of Syrian military intelligence. Malki was murdered by an army sergeant, who was accused of having been in the pay of Syrian sympathizers of the rightist, anti-communist PPS group.

After Malki's death, Serraj became the strong, driving force in the army. He cooperated closely with Hourani. The two slowly but surely swung both Parliament and the army towards a neutralist line and away from cooperation with the West. Gradually, they managed to either oust or condemn most of their leading political opponents as "imperialist spies" or "traitors." The civilians, from President Kuwatly down, wielded less power, as once more army officers and Hourani controlled the situation. On August 6, 1957, the Syrian mission to Moscow received promises of arms and economic assistance from Russia. This mission was headed by Khaled el Azm, then defence minister.

Of all the Arab states, Syria became the closest to Russia. The world came close to an international conflagration when Syria, supported by Russia, accused Turkey and America of wanting to invade Syria. In that year of tension, the main topics became "sputnik" and Syria.

XXI
Chain Reaction in Lebanon

It was tough everywhere in the Middle East. In Lebanon, Syria's neighbor, the leaders stared uneasily at the happenings in Damascus. On several occasions, Syrian officers had told their Lebanese opposite numbers that the time had come for them to take over control of their country.

In a country where the population was almost evenly divided between Christians and Muslims, the problem of maintaining peace and harmony was a delicate, almost impossible one. Yet the shrewd, balanced reign of President Beshara el Khoury managed to keep Lebanon stable despite some difficult moments.

When an economic dispute arose between Syria and Lebanon, many of the Lebanese Muslims tended to side with the Syrians, regardless of whether it was to the best interests of Lebanon or not. But beside President El Khoury, himself a Christian, was a colourful, powerful, and astute Muslim, Premier Riad Solh.

The two guided their tiny nation through the maze of intrigues.

There were other elements at play. Communists made Lebanon their Middle Eastern headquarters. Supporters of the Greater Syria plan worked underground. The Syrian National Party, favoring a union of a republican regime grouping Syria and Lebanon, intrigued against the existing regime.

When Antoun Saadeh, a Lebanese Christian who led this movement, tried to stage a coup d'état, he touched off a new uneasy day in which the Lebanese security forces engaged in several gun battles with his followers. Many Syrians favored Saadeh's movement, and when he found he was going to be defeated by the authorities, he escaped and sought refuge in Syria. From there his followers kept infiltrating into Lebanon and skirmishing with the police and army.

But with the changing regime in Syria, the leaders made a deal, and Saadeh was deported to Lebanon. In a lightning trial he was sentenced to death and shot by a firing squad. His followers, however, who then included many prominent Syrians, kept up the underground movement in Lebanon.

In 1951, while Riad Solh was visiting King Abdullah in Amman, followers of Saadeh shot and killed the Lebanese leader. Thus Lebanon, and the Arab world in general, lost one of its cleverest leaders.

The powerful Khoury-Solh team was split by death. It was not long after that a small group of deputies, disgusted by the deteriorating situation, organized a general strike throughout Lebanon. Among these deputies were Camille Chamoun, Hamid Franjieh, Kamal Jumblatt, and others.

They called on the people to strike and paralyze everything in the country until Pres. Beshara el Khoury resigned. Beirut and the mountains of Lebanon shut down tight for three days. When El Khoury asked Gen. Fuad Shehab, the chief of staff of the Lebanese army, to shoot on peaceful demonstrators, the general refused to relay this command to the soldiers.

Shehab told El Khoury he could not order Lebanese soldiers to fire on Lebanese citizens who were protesting against the corruption that had flooded Lebanon. El Khoury realized he had no alternative but to resign. He did and handed General Shehab the reins of power.

It is to the credit of General Shehab that he did not follow the example of other military leaders in the various Middle Eastern countries and take over the country. Right from the start he made it clear that he was determined to hand over the government to civilian politicians again. He could have stayed in power as president and such was his popularity that no one would have objected. Instead, he asked Parliament to elect a new president.

The two leading contenders were Camille Chamoun and Hamid Franjieh. They sounded out the deputies to see who stood a better chance of being voted president.

When the unofficial count indicated that Chamoun would get it, Franjieh announced his withdrawal from the presidential race. The new regime wanted to have the president unanimously elected by Parliament. Harmony was not to remain long between the men who had staged this bloodless coup in Lebanon. Right from the start, there were rivalries that grew in bitterness between President Chamoun and his erstwhile allies.

XXII
Jordanian Drama

Four days after the assassination of Riad Solh, the Arab world got another shock. While leaving the Haram el Sherif in Jerusalem, King Abdullah was shot and killed. The subsequent trial condemned a group of Palestinian Arabs and the self-exiled Col. Abdullah el Tel, formerly commander of the Transjordanian forces in Jerusalem during the Palestine war. El Tel had been living in Cairo where he had gone after charging that King Abdullah was a mere toy in the hands of Glubb Pasha, the then British chief of staff of the Arab Legion.

The Jordanian court sentenced El Tel to death in absentia. The actual killer of the old king had been riddled by the bullets of Abdullah's bodyguard. Three others were hanged for being found guilty of planning the assassination of the colorful desert monarch.

When the old king died, Jordan was immediately thrown into a chaotic crisis. The crown prince, Talal ben Abdullah, was in a sanatorium in Switzerland. He was subject to various mental illnesses and had been under treatment for some time. It was an open secret that Abdullah had preferred his younger son, Prince Naif, to Talal. Many said that Abdullah favored making either Naif, or Hussein, Talal's son as the next king.

When bullets unexpectedly ended Abdullah's life, Hussein was still a schoolboy. Naif was immediately proclaimed regent. There was considerable speculation that Naif was plotting to seize the throne, and columns were written about it.

I flew to Amman after having obtained special clearance from the prime minister in Jordan. Such was the situation and fear of a coup from outside that the Jordanians had sealed themselves inside their country. The Bedouin Jordanians were on a rampage. Their king had been killed by Palestinian Arabs, and they were out for vengeance. The Palestinians quietly stayed indoors and prayed that Glubb Pasha and his Arab Legion could hold back the mob. A few years later, those who had stayed indoors had become strong enough to control the streets and riot to get Glubb thrown out of Jordan.

At the palace, I had a long talk with Naif. The husky, young Arab prince was visibly still shaken by his father's murder and the responsibilities that had been thrust upon him. It was also quite obvious that many intriguers were trying to get him to demand the throne. After the usual preliminaries, I asked him whether it was true that he intended to become king. He shook his head and told me that he wished I could make it clear publicly that he had no intention of doing anything of the sort. His elder brother, Talal, was king, and Hussein, his crown prince. As soon as Allah gave Talal his health, he, Naif, would step down.

Supposing Talal remained sick? Naif rang the bell and asked the Circassian guard to bring in young Prince Hussein. The young man walked into the office, still pale and shaken—he had been beside his grandfather when Abdullah was shot. Gravely he shook hands and, with a poise far older than his years, accepted my condolences.

Naif put his arm around his nephew's shoulders and swore by all that was holy that should God see fit to keep Talal ill, then he would serve his nephew Hussein, the rightful heir to the throne.

The drama did not end there. Talal recovered enough to be crowned king, only to suffer a relapse shortly after during a visit to Europe. From Paris he was whisked to Lausanne. His wife,

Queen Zein, had gone there with her children to escape from Talal, who was subject to dangerous fits.

Talal and his suite remained at the Beau Rivage at Ouchy while Zein was in hiding. As the news spread that Talal was hopelessly deranged, Lausanne became the site of Middle Eastern intrigue. Leading politicians from every Arab capital came to Switzerland to see how they could divide the spoils. From Iraq, Premier Nuri es Said came for a "holiday." Syria sent its elder statesman, Fares el Khoury. Prince Naif turned up from Amman and so did Premier Tewfick Aboul Hoda. Lebanon and Egypt had observers on the spot. Each and every one had some scheme he was trying to promote. The Iraqis were reported to feel that this would be a good time to unite Iraq and Jordan by placing the two countries under the regency of Prince Abdul Ilah of Iraq.

Premier Aboul Hoda, who told me this report, said he was doing everything in his power to prevent the king from signing away his kingdom. Naif was there, once again seeing whether he could get into the picture. Syria wanted to see whether it could not unite Jordan and Syria. The Egyptians insisted that Talal was perfectly sane and that this was all a British plot because Talal was anti-British.

The soft-spoken Aboul Hoda finally got the upper hand. He managed to convince the king that he should return to Jordan. At lunch, on the eve of their departure, Aboul Hoda told me that it looked fairly hopeless for the king. But he was determined to get him away from the intrigues of the various Arab politicians and settle this matter between Jordanians. Talal had agreed that it would be better for him to be separated from his wife and children. The idea that he had tried to harm them during his fits tortured him in his moments of lucidity.

That afternoon, Talal was in the garden of the hotel, watched at a discreet distance by his guards as he walked with his children. He played with them and often picked up the youngest in a fit of pathetic affection. That evening Talal boarded a train for Italy and home. A few days later, he had abdicated in favor of his son.

XXIII
Revolution in Egypt

In Egypt, on October 6, 1951, Nahas Pasha's Wafdist government had abrogated the Anglo-Egyptian treaty of 1936, and Egyptian guerillas had started operations in the Suez Canal area. Thousands of British fighting men had been rushed to the British bases in the Canal zone to repel the growing Egyptian resistance. Hardly a day went by without some clash and some casualty. It was obvious that a showdown was coming and that traffic through the Suez Canal was threatened. More British troops were rushed to the Canal zone and took over complete control from the Egyptian authorities.

From October to January, the guerilla activities against the British increased. All Egyptian workers—over sixty thousand—working in British camps, walked out, and the British forces were becoming tougher. There were occasional riots in Cairo, but the main scene of activity was the "Zone" as the Suez Canal area was called.

There is no doubt that the Wafdist government had precipitated the crisis with Britain to cover up its deficiencies in the internal front where they were facing more and more criticisms by their handling of social reforms and the increasing corruption and rocketing cost of living. To divert the attention of the masses and prevent their getting dismissed from power, they staged their dramatic abrogation of the Anglo-Egyptian treaty and rejected the four-power proposals sent by the United States, Britain, Turkey, and France for a Middle East defense pact.

While the Wafdists were passing new laws permitting any Egyptian to carry arms and supervising the training of volunteers for a "liberation army," other tycoons were playing havoc with Egyptian cotton to the detriment of Egypt's financial situation but to their own personal benefits. Corruption, graft, and nepotism reached a new high while the average Egyptian had his eyes focused on the Suez Canal zone.

British slowness to feel the pulse of the people brought Egypt to the edge of the precipice. No matter what were the faults of Egypt's rulers, there is no doubt that there was unanimous feeling of antagonism, even hatred, against Britain. The British adopted a shortsighted policy in Egypt. They were too tough. Centurion tanks were used against pop guns by untrained Egyptian guerillas. Villages were combed and some were destroyed.

On January 25, General Erskine, commanding British troops in Egypt, surrounded the governorate and government sanitary building at Ismailia, where Egyptian police were quartered, and gave them a few minutes to lay down their arms and surrender. He charged them with sheltering guerillas and even participating in operations against the British troops. From his comfortable quarters in Cairo, cigar-smoking minister of the Interior, Fouad Sarag el Din Pasha, told the policemen to resist to the last bullet.

There were about one thousand eight hundred British troops supported by Centurion tanks and mortars around the two buildings. Inside there were about four hundred Egyptian policemen and auxilliaries. British tanks fired a blank shell as a warning to surrender. The nervous, trigger-happy, besieged Egyptians immediately opened up with their rifles and small arms. After a while, the British blazed away with mortars, the Centurions, and small arms.

The one-sided fight did not last long—about three hours. The British had a handful of casualties. On the Egyptian side, were over fifty dead and one hundred fifty wounded before the courageous Egyptian officer, spattered with blood, came out with his men. The British paid due homage to the bravery of the Egyptians and whisked off the wounded to army hospitals. The rest were interned.

In my opinion, Serag el Din did a wicked thing in ordering the poorly equipped policemen to defend themselves against British tanks and guns and trained paratroopers. The British decision to send tanks smashing through the brickwork to crush the Egyptians was even more wicked and demonstrated a frame of mind that should have changed a long time ago. It would have been just as easy to besiege the Egyptians and starve them out, by cutting their water and food supplies.

But presumably, the British had decided on a show of force to tell the world that the tail of the British lion could not be twisted with impunity. In the past, such actions might have been successful, but Erksine's riding roughshod over the Egyptians left a bad taste in the mouths of even the British troops carrying out his orders. It smacked too much of Nazi tactics. It did not contribute to encourage the Middle East to accept democracy as a fine thing, if this was the interpretation of democracy. To a confused group of young nations, just emerging from centuries of subjugation and in whose minds definitions are not yet clear, Erskine's action was a setback to the West.

Yet the Ismailia incident served a purpose. It convinced many people, both Egyptians and foreigners, that the Egyptian had courage and when defending something in which he believed, could fight well. Those Egyptian policemen did not fight just because Serag el Din Pasha ordered it. They fought because they were getting tired of being pushed around. So they fought well.

The reaction to Erskine's Ismailia charge followed immediately. On January 26, the auxilliary police in Cairo mutinied, marched out of their barracks, went to Fuad el Awal University, and joined the students they had previously held in control. Thousands marched through the streets demanding war on Britain, vengeance against the British, and immediate action by the authorities.

By midday, the situation was chaotic. Crowds started to set fire to cafes, cinemas, places of entertainment, shops, and buildings. Foreign-owned establishments went up in flames. The police did not interfere. The fire brigade had all its hoses cut. The American-owned Metro cinema, British-owned Rivoli, the Swiss-owned Groppi food stores, world-famous Shepherd's Hotel, and dozens of other places were set on fire. Smoke curled over the capital as hordes, carrying torches, sped through the main streets of the capital. Terrified inhabitants hid in their flats and wondered whether soon the masses would crash into homes.

In Barclay's Bank, some of the staff were trapped in the vaults and died. At the Turf Club, several Englishmen were killed or wounded by the hate-filled crowd. The Swedish consulate was burned. There was undoubtedly some organisation behind all this, but once it had started, it snowballed into chaos as the mobs joined the organized bands. There was more arson and looting.

By the afternoon, the Egyptian army was ordered to restore order. Martial law was declared by the Wafdist government and a curfew imposed.

The next day, King Farouk dismissed the Wafdists, charging them with negligence in government and failure to maintain security. There is no doubt the army saved the day in Cairo.

The king asked Ali Maher Pasha, seventy-two-year-old politician, to form a new cabinet and restore order in the country. Maher Pasha had twice been premier in difficult times. Nahas Pasha had interned him during the war. He would do a good job.

Almost everybody expected Maher Pasha to go for the Wafdists by dissolving the Chamber of Deputies and charging many of the former government of corruption and negligence. Maher started right away by reassuring the Wafdists he had no such intentions. He intended keeping on the Chamber and consulting all parties in the important steps he intended to take. He called Nahas Pasha his "illustrious predecessor."

Maher Pasha's friends said he was following the policy of the iron fist in the velvet glove. Others believed that his diplomatic subtleties were useless with the Wafdists and the present mood of the people.

Exactly one month later, Naguib el Hilaly Pasha, one-time Wafdist who had been dismissed from the party because he had openly attacked the corruption of his fellow Wafdists, was brought in as new premier. Maher Pasha had not pleased many people by his policy, and he was placed in such a position that obliged him to resign.

Hilaly brought with him an independent team of technicians and announced his firm intention of fighting two problems simultaneously—the internal corruption and the Anglo-Egyptian problem. He felt that they were one and the same problem. Without internal stability and cleanliness, Egypt had neither the right nor the capacity to achieve full independence, he said.

The new premier struck me as being sincere and clever. His reputation as one of the cleverest lawyers of the land and his unquestionable honesty were two important factors in his favor. He tackled the Egyptian problem as it had never been tackled before, purging corruption while negotiating with the British. He made a lot of enemies and right from the start, they tried to make trouble. There were demonstrations at the university and plots were being worked out. His tough, young minister of interior, Mortada el Maraghy, quelled all troubles firmly.

When it was clear that the government was brooking no nonsense, people settled down, if somewhat critically, to see what Hilaly would do. They would give him a chance, but most of them doubted whether he would succeed, either in reaching a satisfactory agreement with Britain or purging the country from corrupt officials.

Hilaly, however, did not last long. He resigned on June 30 and was replaced by Hussein Sirry Pasha, a veteran politician, well-liked by many who did not want Hilaly's anticorruption purge to continue.

Meanwhile, it was becoming obvious to many that the army was starting to have ideas. People started hearing about the Free Officers movement and of the silent struggle within the army. It was no secret that among Farouk's favorite generals was one Maj. Gen. Hussein Sirry Amer. In December 1951, Amer was appointed commander of the Frontier Corps, one of Egypt's best-trained forces. He replaced a man who was little known outside Egyptian army circles at the time—Gen. Mohammed Naguib.

General Naguib had distinguished himself during the Palestine campaign as the only senior officer who had been wounded in action. He was an honest, likable man and extremely popular among the younger officers. His transfer from the Frontier Corps drew a lot of criticism.

Not long later, in the early days of 1952, the Free Officers backed Naguib's nomination as president of the Officers' Club, built by Farouk to keep the officers happy. It was well known at the time that the palace nominee was Amer. Fearing defeat, the king tried to postpone the elections, but the manoeuver was ignored. Naguib was elected president of the club, and the first public defiance of the army against the king caused comment in every café in Egypt.

For many, this was the handwriting on the wall, even more so than the burning of Cairo. But Farouk was a stubborn man, and he reacted by dissolving the Officers' Club committee and later by trying to get Sirry Pasha to appoint General Sirry Amer as minister of War. Sirry resigned.

Again, Farouk turned to Hilaly Pasha, and it is said that he promised him carte blanche in his purges. The new government did not last twenty-four hours. The Free Officers staged their revolution and took over Egypt in a matter of hours on July 23, 1952. They brought back Ali Maher as premier, forced Farouk to abdicate and sail away to Capri and exile on July 26th.

Within a matter of a month, Naguib and Nasser ruled Egypt, with Gamal Abdel Nasser being the real strongman of the new regime. It was only later that the world discovered that Naguib had never really been a member of the Free Officers' movement but had been invited to head it as an older man in whom the masses would have confidence.

This amazing leader soon had a record that shook the world. Having ousted Farouk, he then dismissed Naguib, abolished the monarchy and instituted a republican regime in Egypt. Soon, Nasser captured the imagination of the Arab world. Many of his subsequent moves shook the entire world and caused his name to be the topic of conversation in the capitals of all the great powers.

XXIV
Abdel Nasser and the Arabs

This officer who rose from a lower middle class family to become the most powerful man in the Arab world is a true son of Egypt. Many have said that for the first time in over four thousand years, Egypt was being ruled by a real native of the land, and not by a man of foreign origin.

From early life, Abdel Nasser rebelled against the existing regimes in Egypt and most especially against the British occupation of his country. As an officer, he plotted for ten years before he was able to stage his revolt that overthrew Farouk, the monarchical system in Egypt, and forced out the British from the Suez Canal zone.

He worked hard at his conspiracy against Farouk. Often he spent nights plotting with his fellow-officers. Some years before he came to power, a fussy school teacher who lived near the Abdel Nassers warned his wife that the young officers—meaning Gamal Abdel Nasser—often spent their nights gambling and carousing. She advised the quiet young wife to put her foot down.

After Abdel Nasser came to power, he inspected a school and recognized his former neighbor at the receiving line. As he shook hands, he remarked to her, "You see, I wasn't spending my nights gambling."

Of course, it was gambling but of a totally different nature. Abdel Nasser was gambling when he started the revolution. He kept on gambling after that. He gambled when he made an arms deal with Russia and Czechoslavakia, and he gambled again when he nationalized the Suez Canal.

In and out of the Middle East, some people have admired him for his acts, while others have cursed him. He has been called dictator, and he has been condemned as the man who paved the way for Russia in the Middle East. When he nationalized the Suez Canal, many nations of the world shouted that he had no respect for international agreements and that such a leader should not be allowed to continue in power.

Yet, most of the major acts in his career that were condemned by the West have been hailed by the Arabs. When he reached an arms agreement with the communists, it was a measure of extreme desperation. The Israelis had launched several reprisal raids against the Gaza strip. People will argue that the raids had been in retaliation for several ''fedayin'' raids organized by the Egyptians. However, this was no excuse for Israel to take the law into its own hands. The raids were ruthless and thorough. Abdel Nasser asked for arms, and the West refused. If anything has antagonized the Arabs during the past fifteen years, it is the constant feeling that the Western world has sided with Israel against the Arabs, while often admitting the injustice of Zionist claims.

So when Nasser announced his arms deal with Russia and Czechoslovakia, the Arabs hailed it as wonderful news, despite the underlying fear of some that this could establish a very dangerous precedent. But those who felt this way about it dared not utter a word, so great was public jubilation.

Nasser became a giant from the moment he went to Bandoeng to attend the Afro-Asian gathering. He was easily the most dashing of the leaders there, and Nehru and Chou en Lai lionized him.

Not all the Arabs liked the role that Nasser played, but like it or not, they all realized that he had assumed world stature. Many tried to cut him to size, while in turn, he was determined to play the role he considered was his—to unite the Arab world under Egyptian leadership.

The most amazing international blunder was the three-nation war against Egypt. First, Israel struck across the Gaza Strip, and then British and French forces landed at Port Said and advanced along the Suez Canal. There were some who may have condemned an Anglo-French attack against Egypt on the grounds that Nasser had grabbed the Suez Canal—although even that was hard to justify. But what was about the most stupid mistake committed by France and Britain was to join Israel in such a military expedition. What little prestige they may have enjoyed disappeared.

The Arabs accused the two European powers of collusion with Israel and disbelieved any denials. Nasser's forces retreated and the three attackers grabbed hold of virtually the entire Sinai peninsula, and a good part of the Canal. But what started as a military victory for them turned into a bitter political defeat.

Nasser emerged from this short war as a hero in the eyes of most of the Arabs. Oil pipelines in Syria had been cut, and the Arab world in general became very hostile, in varying degrees.

For a while, Western Europe was desperately short of oil supplies, proof, if any was needed, of the importance at that time of the Arab world to European economy.

Nasser continued to state that Arab nationalism's best policy was to avoid all military pacts and to adhere to "positive neutralism." He blasted Iraq for having formed the Baghdad pact with Turkey, Pakistan, Iran, and Britain. The United States, which had contributed considerably to the idea of this "northern tier" grouping, did not fully join.

At one time, Nasser had grouped around him, in an Arab military pact, Syria, Saudi Arabia, Jordan, and Yemen. They all criticized Iraq but failed to shake Premier Nuri el Said from power. Egypt, particularly, with its powerful radio broadcasts and its well-organized propaganda, did its best. Iraq retaliated by exposing the Egyptian military attaché as having plotted to carry out terrorist acts in Iraq, and expelled him.

In Jordan, young King Hussein, stirred by young officers and by his own undeniable nationalist feelings, removed the almost legendary Glubb Pasha from his post as chief of staff of the Arab Legion of Jordan. His closest advisors at the time were young officers led by Aly Abu Nuwar, who quickly rose from captain to Major General and replaced Glubb as chief of staff.

Not too long after, Hussein realized that Nuwar and the socialist premier, Soleiman el Nabulsi, were planning to overthrow him. Jordan went through a period of riots, demonstrations, and army plots. Hussein reacted with amazing courage and firmness. He rallied the army around him, and contemptuously allowed the frightened Abu Nuwar to leave the country.

People kept on asking where young Hussein had gathered enough strength and decision to deal so confidently with a situation that would have unnerved older men. From early childhood, Hussein had shown the same qualities that his grandfather, Abdullah, had possessed. When people asked me who had been behind the young monarch at the time, I used to answer, "The ghost of his grandfather."

Hussein realized that Nasser was against him and in favor of Abu Nuwar and Nabulsi. From that moment on, he broke with Egypt. There were other occasions after Abu Nuwar's dismissal, when Egypt tried to provoke trouble for Hussein, charging him with treason against Arab nationalism, but Hussein held firm and gave as much as he received.

During the Abu Nuwar crisis, when Syrian and Saudi forces were inside Jordan and Israel seriously considering grabbing Arab Jerusalem and the West Bank of Jordan, the United States came out in full support of Hussein. The Sixth Fleet steamed to the eastern Mediterranean to back Hussein. In many parts of the Arab World, many immediately protested that this was a new sort of "gunboat diplomacy." The Arabs, claimed these critics, wanted to get rid of Hussein who was being kept in power by American warships and guns. In point of fact, the presence of the Sixth Fleet probably saved the West Bank from being occupied by Israel. It was mainly to Israel that America's warning was directed to keep hands off Jordan.

Another vital development occurred during that spring of 1957. King Saud, who had previously backed Nasser to the hilt, started having second thoughts about the matter. He felt that Arab kings were being threatened and did not like the growing communist menace in the area. He sided with King Hussein against Egypt and Syria, his erstwhile allies. It was only natural for King Saud to feel that the best stability resided in the respect of kings and that once Hussein went, it would be a matter of time before other Arab kings would go. Saud was especially worried by developments in Syria.

At first imperceptibly, and later quite obviously, Syria was not only following Egypt's lead in dealings with the Iron Curtain countries but actually overpassed Egypt. Syria brought arms, technicians, and made huge economic deals with Russia. Politically, they tended more and more to follow the Moscow line and adopted a policy that was far more leftist than Nasser's. Moderate officers were replaced by extreme nationalists and some suspected communists. The dividing line, among many Syrians, between communism and Arab nationalism disappeared. The two blended into one and, because of this, other Arab nationalists worried. Even Nasser was not happy, but there was little he could do to check the Syrian rush towards the Kremlin. The Syrians maintained that they were not communists, and only the Western powers were to blame if the Arabs turned to Russia for friendship and aid. They accused the Americans of plotting against Syria and charged that such countries as Jordan, Iraq, and Lebanon were run by stooges of American imperialism. Their criticism of King Saud was more moderately worded, but the Syrians were plainly unhappy at Saud's pro-American stand.

Gradually, the fight developed until the Arabs were pitted against each other. Egypt and Syria stood together, against Iraq, Jordan, Lebanon, and Saudi Arabia. In many of these countries, public opinion, such as it was, was divided. Anti-Nasser governments found that Nasser was still a hero in the eyes of many people in the countries concerned, while inside Syria there were many who resented the leftist rule. In Egypt, Nasser's popularity rose and fell, depending on circumstances.

Those Arabs who feared communism believed that strife would continue in the Arab world, so long as the Western powers did not produce some satisfactory solution to the Arab-Israeli problem, which basically is at the root of all the crises in the Arab world. So long as Russia was represented as the Arabs' friend and supplier, then many identified nationalism with communism, or at least, with a pro-Russian policy.

Whether the Western powers liked it or not, Russia had entered the Middle Eastern political field, actively and aggressively. All efforts had previously been repulsed, but by 1957, the Soviets had established a political foothold in the area and were pushing hard.

Subsequent developments in the Arab world have happened too recently to be seen in proper perspective. Only history will condone or condemn the acts of various leaders.

The Middle East, more than any other part of the world, had once again become—as it has often been through history—the main area of tension, the center of chaos.